BEST of the BEST
from
TENNESSEE

Selected Recipes from Tennessee's
FAVORITE COOKBOOKS

BEST
of the BEST
from
TENNESSEE

Selected Recipes from Tennessee's
FAVORITE COOKBOOKS

EDITED BY
Gwen McKee
AND
Barbara Moseley

Illustrated by Tupper Davidson

QUAIL RIDGE PRESS

CONTENTS

Visitors to the Homeplace find the farm "family" busy about their chores of an 1850s farm. Land Between the Lakes.

PREFACE

The Tennessee kitchen is not only a place where good food is prepared, but a place of meeting and sharing, whether it is in an elegant townhouse in the city or a humble log cabin in the mountains. It is our hope that the pages within will take you on a tasting tour of Tennessee, from Johnson City to Memphis, from Chattanooga to Clarksville. The 54 Tennessee cookbooks represented here come from all over the state, giving a wide representation of the Volunteer State's style of cooking.

The natural resources of Tennessee have accounted for the basic simplicity of its fare—the corn from its fields, the apples from its orchards, the fish from its streams. The recipes created by the original settlers have been handed down from generation to generation, with modern methods helping to improve old family favorites. Tennesseans are basically "down-home folks" who take pride in their heritage. This cookbook is for those who want a taste of "going back home." Within these pages are recipes which can evoke the kind of memories and feelings associated with simple food served with love and pride as it has been for generations in Tennessee.

We are grateful to the 54 contributing cookbook authors, editors, and publishers whose cooperation and assistance were vital to the development of the book. Each of the contributing cookbooks has its own unique features and flavor. We have attempted to retain this flavor by reproducing the recipes as they appear in each book, changing only typeset style for uniformity. A complete catalog of these contributing cookbooks begins on page 269. We do beg forgiveness for any books that might have been included that we inadvertently overlooked.

Our thanks to the food editors from newspapers all over the state who recommended cookbooks for inclusion; to the many book-store and gift shop managers who lent us their knowledge of popular books in their area; and to the beautiful people who gave us their opinions and recommendations and smiles all along the way through friendly Tennessee.

We are greateful to the kind folks at the Tennessee Department of Tourist Development who gave us access to their abundance of photos and information. And thanks to Tupper Davidson for beautifully capturing the flavor of Tennessee in her charming drawings.

Since traveling all over the state, sampling its native cooking along the way, experiencing its cultural history, and getting to know its friendly people, a little bit of Tennessee's pride has rubbed off on us. We take great pride in sharing these wonderful recipes from the leading cookbooks in the beautiful state of Tennessee.

Gwen McKee and Barbara Moseley

CONTRIBUTING COOKBOOKS

. . . and garnish with Memories
The Apple Barn Cookbook
Change of Seasons
Chattanooga Cook Book
Cookin' & Quiltin'
Cracker Barrel Old Country Stores: Old Timey Recipes &
Proverbs to Live By
Das Germantown Kochbuch
Dinner on the Diner
Dixie Delights
Elvis Fans Cookbook
Elvis Fans Cookbook II
Encore! Nashville
Family Favorites by the Miller's Daughters
Flaunting Our Finest
Gatlinburg Recipe Collection
Gazebo Gala
Grand Tour Collection
Home Cooking in a Hurry
It's Greek to Me!
The James K. Polk Cookbook
Joyce's Favorite Recipes
Kiss My Grits
Koinonia Cooking
Kountry Kooking
A Man's Taste
Maury County Cookbook

Contributing Cookbooks

The Memphis Cookbook
Minnie Pearl Cooks
Miss Daisy Entertains
More Home Cooking in a Hurry
The Nashville Cookbook
Nashville Seasons
NCJW Cookbook
The Original Tennessee Homecoming Cookbook
Our Favorite Recipes
Out of this World
Palate Pleasers
Parties & Pleasures
Party Potpourri
Recipes from Miss Daisy's
Rivertown Recipes
St. Paul Cooks
Sam Houston Schoolhouse Cookbook
The Sevier County Cookbook
Smoky Mountain Magic
Southern Secrets
Tennessee Homecoming: Famous Parties, People & Places
Tennessee's 95 Magic Mixes: Second Helping
Tennessee Treasure
Upper Crust: A Slice of the South
Well Seasoned
Woman's Exchange Cookbook I
Woman's Exchange Cookbook II
World's Fair Cookbook

Appetizers

Beale Street, the birthplace of the blues. Memphis.

Hot Cider Punch

2 cups water
1 tablespoon ginger
1 tablespoon nutmeg
6 whole cloves
6 whole allspice

2 (2-inch) cinnamon sticks
1 gallon apple cider
2 cups sugar
1½ cups brown sugar, firmly
  packed

Combine water and spices in large saucepan; cover and bring to a boil. Boil 10 minutes. Add apple cider and sugar. Simmer over low heat 10 minutes, stirring frequently. Serve hot. Yield: 5 quarts.

The Apple Barn Cookbook

Hot Cranberry Punch

1 (48-ounce) can cranberry juice
  cocktail
1 (48-ounce) pineapple juice,
  unsweetened

⅓–½ cup brown sugar
3 cinnamon sticks
3 teaspoons whole cloves

Put cinnamon sticks, sugar and cloves in top of large coffee maker and allow to process with juices in the coffee pot. Serve hot.

The Sevier County Cookbook

Starlight Three-Fruit Punch

1 (12-ounce) can frozen orange
  juice concentrate, thawed
1 (12-ounce) can frozen
  lemonade concentrate, thawed
1 (46-ounce) can pinapple juice

⅓ cup lemon juice (3 lemons)
2 (12-ounce) bottles ginger ale,
  chilled
2 quarts water

Makes: 1 gallon—30 servings in punch cups.
    "Punch served at the 100th Anniversary of the Assumption Rectory on June 9, 1974."

Das Germantown Kochbuch

Thirst Quencher

1 cup orange juice
1 cup unsweetened pineapple
   juice
¼ cup lemon juice
¼ cup Maraschino cherry juice

1 cup dry Ginger Ale
2 tablespoons honey
1 pint vanilla ice cream
2 tablespoons sliced Maraschino
   cherries

Mix fruit juices and Ginger Ale; add honey; mix well. Chill thoroughly. Add ice cream; stir until blended. Serve in glasses topped with cherry slices. Makes 1½ quarts

Elvis Fans Cookbook

French Mint Tea

3 family-sized tea bags
Enough water to cover well
Handful of fresh, clean mint
Juice of 4 lemons

1 (12-ounce) can frozen orange
   juice
2 cups sugar

In a pot bring to a boil, tea bags, water and mint. Cover and remove from heat. Allow to steep 30 minutes. Remove tea bags and mint by strainer. Add lemon juice, orange juice and sugar. Add enough water to make 1 gallon. Refrigerate. This is refreshing on hot summer days and good for parties. Yields 1 gallon or 16 (8-ounce) servings.

Southern Secrets

Sweet Passion

Galliano

Cointreau

Kahlua

Half and half

Mix in the proportion that tastes good to you, and whip into a creamy froth. I mix equal parts of Galliano, Kahlua, and Cointreau—and then go heavy on the half-and-half.

Joyce's Favorite Recipes

Tumbleweed

2½ ounces light cream

1½ ounces brandy

1½ ounces Tia Maria (no substitutes)

1½ ounces dark crème de cacao

3 teaspoons crushed ice

Vanilla ice cream, to desired thickness

Chocolate curls

In standard size 4-cup blender, combine cream, liqueurs and ice. Fill blender with ice cream. Blend well, adding more ice cream to desired thickness. Garnish with chocolate curls. Yield: 2 servings.

Upper Crust: A Slice of the South

Tennessee Eggnog

12 eggs, separated
1 cup sugar
1 quart Jack Daniels (black label)
¼ cup rum
1 quart coffee cream
1 quart thick cream
Nutmeg

Break eggs and separate. To the yolks add all the sugar at one time and then beat and beat until the mixture is light, thick and smooth or until you can't feel any sugar particles. Add liquor a little at a time, beating vigorously. Add all of rum and beat again. Add coffee cream. Then add the whipped cream by folding in. Lastly add the egg whites beaten stiff by also the folding in process. Let stand to ripen 2 days. Serve in silver punch bowl with a sprinkling of nutmeg. Serves 30.

Tennessee Homecoming: Famous Parties, People & Places

Marnissimo

In 5-ounce crystal Irish coffee glass, layer:

1 large teaspoon sugar
1 ounce Grand Marnier
3 ounces hot black coffee

Fill remainder of glass with whipped cream. Do not mix.

Grand Tour Collection

Hot Chocolate Mix

1 (6-quart) box powdered milk
½ cup powdered sugar
1 cup Nestle's Quik
½ cup Cremora
1 large box instant chocolate pudding
½ cup cocoa

Combine. Store in airtight container. Use ⅓ cup mix to 1 cup hot water. (It's the pudding in this recipe that makes it so rich and good.)

St. Paul Cooks

Vanilla-Coffee Liqueur

1½ cups brown sugar
1 cup sugar
2 cups water
½ cup instant coffee

3 cups vodka
½ vanilla bean or 2 tablespoons
  vanilla extract

Be sure that brown sugar measure is densely packed. Combine the sugars and 2 cups water and boil 5 minutes. Gradually stir in the coffee, using a wire whisk. Cool. Pour into a tall bottle, jar, or jug; add vodka and vanilla; mix thoroughly. Uncover and let stand for at least two weeks, then remove vanilla bean.

Good as after-dinner drink or to pour over ice cream or fruit. Makes about 5 cups.

Joyce's Favorite Recipes

Cafe Mexicano
Your guests won't leave until this is all gone.

12 cups strong coffee
3 ounces chocolate syrup
¼ cup sugar
½ teaspoon cinnamon

¼ teaspoon nutmeg
1½ cups coffee liqueur
Whipped cream
Cinnamon

Perk the coffee and remove the basket of the percolator. Add syrup, sugar, cinnamon, and nutmeg, stirring to dissolve. Add the liqueur. If not serving immediately, stir occasionally. Serve topped with whipped cream and a dusting of cinnamon. Yield: 12 servings. Preparation time: 20 minutes

Note: This can be doubled or tripled, depending on the size of your coffee pot.

Encore! Nashville

Cheese Puffs

½ loaf unsliced regular bread
8 ounces cream cheese
¼ pound unsalted margarine
⅛ teaspoon paprika
⅛ teaspoon Worchestershire
  sauce
⅛ teaspoon dill weed
2 shakes Tabasco sauce
2 egg whites, beaten

Cut crust from bread; slice bread into 1-inch cubes. Melt cream cheese and unsalted margarine over low heat. Stir to blend. Add spices and sauces. Fold in beaten egg whites.

Dip each bread cube into cream cheese mixture to coat and place on cookie sheet. Bake at 375° for 20 minutes or until golden brown. If desired, freeze and bake later. Yield: 50 puffs. Serving: 1 puff-45 milligrams sodium; 40 calories

Tip: The sodium content of this appetizer is negligible if low-sodium bread is used.

Change of Seasons

Cheese Puffs

2 cups grated plain American
  cheese
2 tablespoons flour
Salt and pepper to taste
2 egg whites, well beaten

Mix cheese with flour and seasonings. Fold into egg whites, roll into little balls with wet hands. Fry in deep fat. A little sausage or ham in the center is great!

Tennessee Homecoming: Famous Parties, People & Places

Hot Cheese Puffs

2 cups (8 ounces) shredded
  sharp cheese
½ cup butter or margarine
1 cup self-rising flour
1 cup chopped dates
½ cup chopped walnuts

Mix cheese and butter; stir in flour until blended. Add dates and nuts. Shape into balls, place on ungreased baking sheet. Bake at 375° for 15 to 20 minutes. Yield: 5 dozen.

Flaunting Our Finest

Cheese Olives

25 ripe olives, pitted
2–3 green onions, minced
½ cup flour
¼ teaspoon salt
⅛ teaspoon mustard

4 ounces sharp Cheddar cheese
3 tablespoons butter, melted and
  cooled slightly
1 tablespoon milk
1–2 drops Tabasco

Stuff olives with onion. Blend flour with salt, mustard, and shredded cheese. Stir into mixture the butter, milk and Tabasco. Using 1 teaspoon dough per olive, wrap dough around olive, place on baking sheet. Bake at 400° for 10 to 12 minutes. Yield: 25 canapes.

These may be placed in foil pan and frozen. Very handy for unexpected guests. Stuffed green olives may be substituted.

Woman's Exchange Cookbook I

Pineapple Cheese Ball

2 (8-ounce) packages cream
  cheese, softened
1 (8½-ounce) can crushed
  pineapple, drained
2 cups chopped pecans

¼ cup green pepper, finely
  chopped
2 tablespoons onion, finely
  chopped
1 tablespoon seasoned salt

In medium bowl with fork, mix cream cheese until smooth. Stir in pineapple, one cup pecans, green pepper, onion and seasoned salt. Shape into ball and roll in remaining nuts. Wrap in foil; refrigerate overnight. To serve, place cheese on board, garnish with pineapple slices and cherries, if desired. Surround with different crackers.

Elvis Fans Cookbook

Gatlinburg is a charming town called "The Gateway to the Smokies." With more than 300 shops, it may well have the largest concentration of working craftspeople in the South. Above Gatlinburg is Ober Gatlinburg, where winter sports—including snow skiing—are enjoyed year round.

Chutney Cheese Ball

1 (8-ounce) package cream
  cheese
¼ to ½ cup chutney (mango is
  good)
½ cup chopped toasted almonds

¼ teaspoon dry mustard
1 teaspoon curry powder
Chopped walnuts (optional)

Bring cream cheese to room temperature to facilitate creaming. Place in bowl along with chutney, almonds, mustard and curry. Combine with a fork or pastry blender and form into a ball or roll. Cover with chopped nuts if desired. Wrap in Saran Wrap and keep in refrigerator until serving time. Serve with variety of crackers.

Grand Tour Collection

Party Snack Fried Cheese Grits

1 teaspoon salt
4 cups water
1 cup quick grits
1 cup sharp Cheddar cheese,
   grated

1 egg, beaten
Dash of hot sauce and paprika

Bring salted water to boil and stir in grits. Cook until grits thicken, remove from heat and add cheese and egg. Stir until cheese melts. Add dash of hot sauce and paprika, if desired. Pour mixture into shallow dish. Cool, then place in refrigerator for several hours (or overnight). Before serving: cut into 1-inch pieces, lightly coat in flour and fry in hot cooking oil until golden. Yield: 36 to 48.

Kiss My Grits

Lena's Oyster Cracker Snacks

1 package Original Hidden
   Valley salad dressing
½ teaspoon dill weed
1 cup Orville Redenbacher
   buttery cooking oil

½ teaspoon onion salt or garlic
   salt
½ teaspoon lemon pepper
1 (11-ounce) package oyster
   crackers

Mix together the packaged dressing, oil, onion or garlic salt, dill weed, and lemon pepper. Pour over the oyster crackers and mix well. Store in air tight containers. Shake well each time before serving.

Maury County Cookbook

Tennessee walking horse farms, where former champions and their offspring can be seen grazing in the rich pastures, cover the rolling hills of south central Tennessee.

Helen's Nuts and Bolts

4 sticks margarine or corn oil
2 level teaspoons garlic salt
2 level teaspoons celery salt
5 teaspoons Worcestershire
  sauce
1 (8-ounce) box Rice Chex
4 ounces Corn Chex

4 ounces Wheat Chex
1 (7-ounce) box Cheerios
1 pound pecan halves
10 ounce pretzel sticks
1 small can party mixed nuts
  (optional)

Melt butter with all seasonings. Mix remaining ingredients in well, using wooden spoon to stir over it. Try to coat evenly. Bake uncovered in 250° oven for 1½–2 hours. Stir every 15 minutes while baking. Let cool overnight in pan that it was baked in.

Our Favorite Recipes

Sausage Pin Wheels

½ pound pork sausage
Few drops of Tabasco sauce
2 cups biscuit mix

2 tablespoons butter or
    margarine
Milk or water

Let sausage warm to room temperature so it will be spreadable; then blend in a few drops of Tabasco sauce. Put biscuit mix into bowl, add butter and work with fork until crumbly. Mix in water or milk as directed on package for biscuits. Roll dough into rectangle; spread sausage evenly and roll up. Wrap and store in refrigerator or freezer. Cut into slices when half-dozen or very cold. Bake on ungreased cookie sheet at 375° for about 15 minutes. Makes about 50 cookie-size pinwheels.

The Sevier County Cookbook

Seafood Canapes
Absolutely wonderful!

1 cup cooked, chopped shrimp
  or crabmeat
1 cup shredded Swiss cheese
2 tablespoons thinly sliced green
  onion
Mayonnaise to bind
½ teaspoon garlic powder

¼ teaspoon curry powder,
  optional
1 package refrigerator
  butterflake dinner rolls
½ cup thinly sliced water
  chestnuts
Chopped parsley for topping

Combine the seafood, cheese, green onion, mayonnaise and seasonings. Separate the rolls into thin rounds and place on a cookie sheet. Top with the shrimp mixture and water chestnuts. Sprinkle with parsley. Bake at 375° for 10 minutes. Yield: 36 canapes.

Note: This may be made ahead and refrigerated, covered.

Out of this World

Cocktail Party Meatballs

8 pounds ground beef
4 cups bread crumbs
½ cup chopped onions
1 teaspoon dry mustard
6 teaspoons salt

½ teaspoon pepper
3 eggs, beaten
1⅓ cups milk
½ cup Crisco

Mix beef, crumbs, onions, mustard, salt, pepper, eggs and milk. Form into balls, about 1 inch in diameter. Brown in Crisco and drain. Makes about 150 balls. In saucepan mix sauce:

4 cups pineapple juice
4 teaspoons ginger
½ cup cornstarch
½ cup soy sauce

2 cups brown sugar
2 teaspoons salt
2 cups vinegar

Cook and stir the sauce until thick. Serve the sauce in a chafing dish and use toothpicks for getting out the balls. Serve hot. This can be made ahead of time and reheated for serving.

Parties & Pleasures

Salmon Ball

1 pound can red or pink salmon
1 (8-ounce) package cream
  cheese (softened)
1 tablespoon lemon juice
2 teaspoons grated onion
1 teaspoon horseradish
¼ teaspoon salt
¼ teaspoon liquid smoke
½ cup chopped pecans
3 tablespoons chopped parsley

Drain, flake and remove bones and skin from salmon. Combine first 7 ingredients and mix well. Chill several hours. Shape into ball and roll in nuts and parsley. Wrap and freeze for later. If salmon is too costly, 2 cans of tuna are just as yummy.

Rivertown Recipes

Ham Balls

1½–2 pounds ham
1½ pounds lean pork
2½ cups soft bread crumbs
3 eggs, beaten
1¼ cups milk

Grind the two meats in food chopper and then the bread. In mixing bowl, beat the eggs and milk. Pour into the meat and bread mixture.

Make into balls about size of golf balls. Use large baking dish or pan. When putting balls into greased pan, pat them down somewhat. Cover with sauce.

SAUCE:
2 cups brown sugar
⅔ cup vinegar
¾ cup water
2 tablespoons prepared mustard

Mix together and pour over ham balls. Cover with lid or aluminum foil. Bake at 350° for 1 hour. Every so often turn balls in the juice to cover. These are delicious for breakfast!!

Family Favorites by the Miller's Daughters

Sauerkraut Balls

1½ cups cooked ham, ground in food chopper
1½ cups corned beef, ground in food chopper
2 cups sauerkraut, drained
1 onion, put through food chopper
3 tablespoons margarine
1 clove garlic, cut up by hand

6 tablespoons flour
2 eggs
1 tablespoon parsley
½ teaspoon Worcestershire sauce
Dash Lawry salt
¾ cup beef stock
2 cups milk + 2½ cups flour makes the batter
Bread crumbs

Grind the following in food chopper; ham, corned beef, sauerkraut, onion.

Sauté the onion in margarine. Add the meats and cut up garlic. Heat well. Stir in 6 tablespoons flour and eggs. Continue to cook, stirring until mixture is well blended. Add sauerkraut. Add the parsley flakes, Worcestershire sauce, Lawry salt, beef stock. This will become quite thick like a paste. Remove from heat and spread the whole mixture onto a cookie sheet to cool. After cooling, refrigerate to chill well. This enables you to handle the shaping of ball much better.

When making the balls, only take out ½ of mix at a time so won't get too warm to handle. After making 1-inch balls, dip them into the batter. Have a large bowl of fine bread crumbs and cover each ball. Finally, have deep fryer with oil hot to fry until golden brown. Drain on paper towels. Delicious! Also these will freeze very well for later use. All you do is let thaw and put into a covered pan and heat, removing lid for a few minutes to make crispy.

Family Favorites by the Miller's Daughters

Egg Roll

SKIN:

1 egg, beaten and divided in half
2 cups flour
¼ cup cornstarch

Enough water to make ½ thickness of pancakes

Make skin by beating ½ egg, flour, cornstarch and enough water to make a thin batter. Strain batter. Cook the skin until it pops away from small skillet. Turn the skin and cook slowly on the other side. The secret to make perfect skins for egg roll is to have small pan hot and lightly greased. Pour batter into pan and then immediately pour out batter that does not adhere to the pan. This will give a thin skin for the egg rolls.

STUFFING:

2 boiled chicken breasts
  (minced)
½ pound boiled shrimp
  (minced)
½ head cabbage (boiled 5
  minutes, drained and minced)

½ teaspoon white pepper
1 teaspoon salt
2 teaspoons shortening

Mix all ingredients for stuffing. Place in each egg roll skin. Roll up skin. Use other ½ egg to seal edges and fry to a golden brown in hot fat.

World's Fair Cookbook

Asparagus Roll-Ups

Trim 12 slices white bread. Roll each slice gently with a rolling pin. Use fresh, thin-sliced bread. Spread with Lime Butter. Place spear of asparagus on bread and roll-up, placing seam side down. Cut in half, slightly butter ends and dip them in chopped parsley.

LIME BUTTER:
1 stick softened butter
1 tablespoon mayonnaise
½ teaspoon lime juice
2 drops green coloring

Mix butter with mayonnaise, lime juice and green coloring. This will produce a pale tint.

Hint: You can make chopped parsley easily. Drop washed parsley in blender with 2 cups of water. Whiz quickly to chop. Drain.

Parties & Pleasures

French Fried Dill Pickle

Dill pickles
½ cup flour
¼ cup beer
1 tablespoon cayenne pepper
1 tablespoon paprika
1 tablespoon black pepper
1 teaspoon salt
2 teaspoons garlic salt
3 dashes Tabasco

Cut dill pickles in slices as thick as a silver dollar. Mix the rest of the ingredients together. Dip pickle slices in batter and quick fry at 375° in grease until the pickle slices float to the top, or about 4 minutes.

A Man's Taste

Hot Crab Dip

8 strips bacon
3 cans crab, drained
2 tablespoons cornstarch
½ can Ro-tel tomatoes, with chives

1 clove garlic
1½ teaspoons dry basil
1 can tomato sauce
4 tablespoons Parmesan cheese

Fry the bacon until crisp, save 4 tablespoons grease in skillet. Add all other ingredients except Parmesan cheese. Salt to taste. Heat and stir until thickened. Add cheese. Serve hot in chafing dish with corn chips.

Parties & Pleasures

Sauce Verte

½ cup chopped, frozen spinach, defrosted and drained
½ cup sour cream
1 cup mayonnaise
1½ tablespoons lemon juice

Salt to taste
3 sprigs parsley, use only leaves
2 green onions, use green tops and bulbs

Place spinach in strainer and drain liquid. Set aside. Place remaining ingredients in blender and blend at high speed until smooth. Combine spinach and blender mixture. Mix well. Refrigerate until ready to use. Serve with cold vegetables as a dip. Yield: 2 cups.

Elvis Fans Cookbook II

Henning is the hometown of author, Alex Haley, and the setting for his acclaimed novel, Roots.

Buried Treasures
Definitely a show-stopper

2 cups mayonnaise
½ cup horseradish, well drained
½ teaspoon monosodium glutamate
2 teaspoons dry mustard
2 teaspoons lemon juice
½ teaspoon salt
1 pound medium shrimp, cooked

1 pint basket small cherry tomatoes
1 (6-ounce) can pitted black olives, drained
1 (8-ounce) can water chestnuts, drained
½ pound whole mushrooms
½ head cauliflower, broken into bite-size florets

Combine mayonnaise with the seasonings. Stir in other ingredients and serve in a shallow bowl with toothpicks. Yield: 8 servings. Preparation time: 15 minutes.

Note: This is best made early in the day or the night before, adding the cauliflower right before serving.

Encore! Nashville

Sea Island Shrimp Spread

1 (3-ounce) package cream
cheese
1 cup sour cream
2 teaspoons lemon juice

1 (0.7-ounce) package Good
Seasons Italian dressing mix
1 (4¼-ounce) can shrimp,
drained and rinsed

Blend ingredients. Let stand at least 4 hours before serving with crackers.

Gazebo Gala

Soups

Originally a water-powered woolen mill (1862), restored Falls Mill now grinds meal and flour for
local farmers. Belvidere.

1886 Cheese Soup

¼ cup butter
½ cup onion, diced
½ cup celery, diced
½ cup carrots, diced
¼ cup all-purpose flour
1½ tablespoons cornstarch
4 cups chicken broth, room temperature

4 cups milk, room temperature
⅛ teaspoon soda
1 pound processed cheese, cubed
1 teaspoon salt
1 teaspoon pepper
⅛ teaspoon cayenne pepper
1 tablespoon dried parsley
Paprika

Melt butter in heavy saucepan. Sauté vegetables until tender. Stir in flour and cornstarch. Cook until bubbly. Add stock and milk gradually, blending into smooth sauce. Add soda and cheese cubes; stir until thickened. Season with salt and peppers, add parsley. Before serving heat thoroughly in double boiler. Do not let boil. Garnish with paprika.

The Original Tennessee Homecoming Cookbook

Potato Cheese Soup

⅓ cup chopped celery
⅓ cup chopped onion
2 tablespoons butter
4 cups pared and diced potatoes
3 cups chicken broth
2 cups milk
1½ teaspoons salt

Dash paprika
¼ teaspoon pepper
2 cups shredded sharp Cheddar
  cheese
French fried onion rings or
  croutons for garnish

In large saucepan, sauté celery and onion in butter until tender. Add potatoes and broth. Simmer until potatoes are tender; stir in milk and seasonings; heat through. Add cheese, stirring until melted. Garnish. Yield: 7½ cups.

Tennessee's 95 Magic Mixes: Second Helping

Potato Soup
(Kartoffelsuppe)

4 slices bacon, diced
3 small cooking onions, finely
  minced
6–8 medium-sized potatoes,
  peeled and diced

½ bay leaf
1 teaspoon paprika
Salt and pepper to taste
1 cup dairy sour cream

Cook bacon over moderate heat until crisp. Remove from the pan and set aside. Cook onions in bacon fat until yellow and transparent, not brown. Add potatoes and bay leaf, cover with boiling water. Cover and cook until the potatoes are tender. Remove bay leaf. Add paprika, salt and pepper. Slowly stir in sour cream and bring to serving temperature. Garnish with crisp bacon bits.

Das Germantown Kochbuch

Cream of Corn Soup
(Tea Room)

1 can cream style corn
1 cup milk
1 cup light cream
2 chicken bouillon cubes or 2
   teaspoons chicken stock base

Salt and white pepper to taste
½ stick butter
Chopped parsley

Blend corn in blender. Combine with milk, cream and bouillon cubes. Add salt and pepper. Pour into saucepan, bring to boil, stirring constantly. Add butter. Garnish with chopped parsley. Serves 4 to 6.

Woman's Exchange Cookbook II

Corn and Ham Chowder

½ cup butter
1 cup chopped celery
½ cup chopped onion
2 cups diced cooked ham
3 (10-ounce) packages frozen
   cream style corn

1½ teaspoons salt
½ teaspoon pepper
½ teaspoon onion salt
½ teaspoon celery salt
1 cup milk

Sauté celery, onion and ham in butter. Add remaining ingredients. Heat. Simmer 20 minutes before serving. Garnish with fresh parsley.

Recipes from Miss Daisy's

Cauliflower Cream Soup

1 medium cauliflower	1½ cups milk
1 chopped onion	Salt and white pepper
1 can cream of chicken soup	Grated Cheddar cheese

Boil cauliflower in salted water until tender. Place in blender and add onion which has been sautéed in butter. Add soup and milk; blend until creamy. Pour into saucepan, heat and add salt and pepper to taste. Sprinkle cheese on top.

Elvis Fans Cookbook

Zucchini Soup

Your guests don't have to know how easy this is.

3 medium zucchini, sliced	1 (8-ounce) package cream
3 tablespoons chopped onion	cheese
4 cups chicken broth	Salt and pepper
¼ teaspoon Italian seasoning	

GARNISH:
Thin lemon slices
Whipped cream

Put zucchini, onion, broth, and seasoning in a deep skillet. Simmer until tender, but not mushy. Blend with cream cheese in a blender or food processor. Take care not to fill blender more than half full when blending ingredients. Add salt and pepper to taste and serve warm. Yield: 4 servings. Preparation time: 30 minutes.

Encore! Nashville

Brimming with Broccoli Soup

1 bunch fresh broccoli, washed
and coarsely chopped
4 cups chicken broth

1 cup Béchamel Sauce
2 egg yolks
2 tablespoons light cream

Cook broccoli in chicken broth until tender. Drain broccoli, reserving liquid, and finely chop in food processor or blender.

BÉCHAMEL SAUCE:

2 tablespoons butter
½ small onion, chopped
2 tablespoons all-purpose flour
½ teaspoon salt

½ teaspoon white pepper
⅛ teaspoon nutmeg
1 cup milk, heated

In large saucepan, melt butter and sauté onion. Add flour and seasonings and stir over low heat until smooth. Add hot milk, stirring until sauce is smooth.

Stir broccoli and all broth into Béchamel Sauce. Mix egg yolks and cream, and add to soup mixture. Mix well and heat. Yield: 6–8 servings.

Dinner on the Diner

Dried Mushroom–Barley Soup

1 cup dried mushrooms	2 tablespoons flour
3 pounds short ribs of beef	1 clove garlic, crushed
Beef marrow bones or veal knuckle	4 carrots, diced fine
1 cup medium barley	4 stalks celery, diced fine
2 onions, diced fine	1 teaspoon salt
1 large can tomatoes, drained and sieved	1 teaspoon freshly ground pepper
3 quarts water	Few drops Tabasco sauce
	2 tablespoons Kitchen Bouquet

Wash mushrooms and soak in warm water to cover for several hours. Drain, saving liquid. Wash and salt meat. Place meat, bones, barley, onions, and tomatoes in water in large soup pot. Bring to a boil, turn low, and simmer covered for 1 hour. Brown flour in a dry iron skillet. Add garlic and stir into hot soup gradually. Add carrots, mushrooms and mushroom liquid, celery, and seasonings. Simmer 1½ hours longer. Add extra water if too thick. Adjust seasoning to taste while cooking. Serves 6 to 8.

NCJW Cookbook

Bean Soup

2 cups dried beans (pinto, navy, blackeyed peas, or kidney beans)

Place beans in a large kettle with water to cover. Bring to a boil and boil 1 hour. Drain off this water and proceed with recipe. To the partially cooked beans add:

8 cups water	2 tablespoons parsley
3 medium-sized onions, chopped	1 ham bone
¼ cup butter	½ teaspoon salt
2 bay leaves	Freshly cracked pepper
1 clove of garlic	

Simmer for 2 hours over very low heat.

Cracker Barrel Old Country Stores:
Old Timey Recipes & Proverbs to Live By

Tamale Lentil Soup

A good friend shared this one-dish meal because she knew how much we enjoy lentils—it is one of our favorites.

½ cup dry lentils
3½ cups water
1 cup frozen whole kernel corn
1 cup frozen cut green beans
1 cup sliced yellow or zucchini squash
1 cup sliced celery
1 clove garlic, minced
Dash pepper
1 cup sliced carrot

1 (8-ounce) can stewed tomatoes
1 can semi-condensed tomato soup
½ cup chopped onion
½ cup chopped green pepper
¾ teaspoon salt
¼ teaspoon ground cumin
¾ teaspoon chili powder
1 recipe Tamale Topper
½ cup shredded Cheddar cheese

In a 4½-quart Dutch oven, combine uncooked lentils and 1½ cups of the water; bring to boiling. Simmer, covered, for 20 minutes or until lentils are softened. Drain. Add the remaining 2 cups water and the remaining ingredients *except* cheese and Tamale Topper. Return to boiling; reduce heat. Simmer, covered, for 20 minutes or until vegetables are almost tender. Drop Tamale Topper by tablespoonful atop soup; cover and simmer about 20 minutes or until topper is done. (Do not lift cover while cooking.) Sprinkle with cheese before serving. Makes 4 servings.

TAMALE TOPPER:
¾ cup cornmeal
½ teaspoon salt
1¼ cups milk

1 egg, beaten
½ cup shredded Cheddar cheese

In saucepan combine cornmeal and salt. Gradually stir in milk. Cook and stir until thickened and bubbly. Stir into 1 beaten egg. Stir in shredded Cheddar cheese.

. . . and garnish with Memories

Tennessee is famous for and deservedly proud of its delicious country hams. After the first hard frost, there is the traditional hog killing in rural Tennessee. After curing, the hams hang in the smokehouse three months, then are put into paper bags for two to three years more.

Lentil and Sausage Soup

1 pound package lentils
7 cups water
2 (16-ounce) cans tomatoes
2 bay leaves
1 tablespoon salt
½ teaspoon pepper

2 pounds Polish sausage
8 bacon slices, diced
1 cup diced carrots
1 medium onion, sliced
1 cup diced celery

Wash lentils and combine with water, tomatoes and seasonings. Bring to boil, reduce heat, add sausage. Cover and simmer for 15 minutes. Fry bacon until slightly limp. Remove all but 1 tablespoon fat from skillet, add carrots, onions and celery to bacon and cook over medium heat 15 minutes, stirring constantly. Add mixture to lentils, continue cooking for 30 minutes. Slice sausage before serving. Yield: 2½ quarts or 8 to 10 servings.

A wonderful winter's night soup.

Woman's Exchange Cookbook II

Chicken Okra Gumbo

2½ or 3 pounds chicken
1 large onion
1 quart canned tomatoes or
  equal amount fresh tomatoes
1 quart canned okra or 1½
  pounds fresh okra

1 small cheesecloth bag filled
  with bay leaves
Salt and pepper

Cut chicken as for frying. Fry until half done. Chop onion and make a roux with flour and the grease from the chicken. Set aside.

Cook chicken in 3 quarts of boiling water until well done. Cut into small pieces, removing all bones. Put into pot and add the tomatoes and okra, cut into small pieces. Add roux and small bag of bay leaves for seasoning. Cook gumbo slowly so that all ingredients will be well done. Usually half a day is necessary to make a good gumbo. Just before serving, season with salt and pepper and remove bay leaves. Gumbo should be served with dry cooked rice. Crabmeat may be added a short time before serving, if desired. Serves 6 to 8 for large portions. Serves 10 for small portions.

The Memphis Cookbook

Chicken and Grits Soup

1 chicken breast	¼ cup dry sherry
2 cups water	1 teaspoon soy sauce
½ teaspoon salt	1 teaspoon sesame oil
2 bay leaves	2 eggs, beaten
1 cup cooked grits	

Cut the chicken breast in half and place the halves in a small sauce pan with the water, salt and bay leaves. Bring the liquid to a boil, cover and simmer for 15 minutes. Remove the chicken to cool. Strain the broth and save. There should be at least 1½ cups of broth; if not, add water. When the chicken is cool, skin it and remove and discard bones. Cut the meat into 1¼-inch cubes. If there is more than 1 cup of chicken meat, keep the excess for another use.

In a 2-quart sauce pan, combine the grits and 1½ cups of the chicken broth; mix and bring to a boil. Reduce heat and add the remainder of chicken and cook for 10 minutes. Stir in the sherry, soy sauce and sesame oil. Remove the saucepan from the heat and add the eggs, blending them in thoroughly. Serve immediately. Serves 4.

Kiss My Grits

Chicken-Noodle Soup

1 (3 pound) chicken, cut up	1 cup sliced carrots
1 tablespoon salt	½ cup chopped onion
Water to cover	½ teaspoon poultry seasoning
1½ cups chopped celery with leaves	2 cups uncooked noodles

Simmer chicken in salted water in covered saucepan until tender. (A frying chicken will take 45 minutes.) Remove chicken from broth; cool enough to handle. Remove skin and bones; chop meat. Skim most fat from broth; measure broth. Add water, if needed, to make 5 cups; bring to boil. Add chicken, vegetables and poultry seasoning. Simmer, covered, 20 minutes. Add noodles; simmer uncovered, 10 minutes or until noodles are tender. Yields 6 servings.

Cookin' & Quiltin'

Oyster Stew

3 cups milk
1 bay leaf
1 rib celery with leaves
1 small onion, peeled and
  quartered
2 sprigs fresh thyme or 1½
  teaspoons dried thyme
12–24 oysters, depending on
  size

¾ cup heavy cream
1 egg yolk
Tabasco sauce to taste
½ teaspoon celery salt
Salt and pepper to taste
2 tablespoons butter
½ teaspoon Worcestershire sauce

Combine the milk, bay leaf, celery, onion, and thyme in a saucepan. Bring just to a boil; but do not boil. Pour the oysters into a deep skillet large enough to hold the stew. Sprinkle with salt and bring to a boil. Cook just until the oysters curl. Strain the milk over the oysters and stir. Discard the solids. Do not boil.

Beat the cream with egg yolk and add Tabasco sauce, celery salt, salt and pepper to taste. Add this to the stew. Bring just to a boil and swirl in butter. Add the Worcestershire sauce and serve piping hot with buttered toast or oyster crackers. This recipe yields four servings.

Joyce's Favorite Recipes

Salads

Apple and apple cider stands are a familiar sight in Tennessee which is so abundant with apple orchards.

Slice of the South Salad

2 (3-ounce) packages blackberry
  gelatin
2 cups blackberries

1 cup pecans, chopped (optional)

Mix gelatin according to package directions. If berries are frozen, decrease cold water to ½ cup, add berries and nuts to gelatin and let chill until set.

TOPPING:

1 (8-ounce) package cream
  cheese, softened
¼ cup milk, cold
½ cup sugar

1 teaspoon vanilla
2 cups whipped topping
Pecans, chopped (optional)

Mix cream cheese with milk, sugar and vanilla; fold mixture into whipped topping. Spread on gelatin and chill. Sprinkle pecans on top as a garnish. Yield: 15 servings.

Upper Crust: A Slice of the South

Cranberry Sour Cream Mold

2 (3-ounce) packages strawberry
  gelatin
1¾ cups boiling water

1 (16-ounce) can jellied
  cranberry sauce
1 cup sour cream

Dissolve gelatin in boiling water. Chill until slightly thickened. Beat cranberry sauce and sour cream together until smooth. Fold into gelatin. Pour into 3-cup mold. Chill until firm. Note: this is a great change from cranberry sauce with your poultry dishes. Jellied whole cranberry sauce may also be used in place of plain.

Dixie Delights

Cranberry Mincemeat Salad

This is exactly the way this fifty-year-old recipe has been handed down. I can see ways to modernize but will give the original.

3 (1-pound) cans cranberry
   sauce, whole or jellied
¾ cup mincemeat

¾ cup chopped walnuts
¾ cup cold water
3 envelopes unflavored gelatin

Crush jellied cranberry sauce with a fork. Stir in mincemeat and nut meats. Measure water in a measuring cup, add gelatin, let stand 2 minutes. Place cup in a pan of boiling water and heat until gelatin is dissolved. Add to cranberry mixture. Chill in one large or 12 individual molds.

. . . and garnish with Memories

Blueberry Salad

2 (3-ounce) boxes concord grape
   flavored gelatin
1 (21-ounce) can blueberry pie
   filling

1 (20-ounce) can crushed
   pineapple
Pecan halves

Dissolve gelatin in 2 cups boiling water; let cool and fold in pie filling and pineapple. Pour into a 9 × 13 × 2-inch pan. Let congeal until firm. Spread topping over congealed mixture. Mark off squares and place pecan on each square. Serves 12.

TOPPING:
1 (8-ounce) package cream
   cheese
1 cup sour cream

1 teaspoon vanilla extract
2 heaping tablespoons sugar

Mix all ingredients together, beating until smooth. Spread evenly over congealed gelatin.

Note: This is also good as a dessert.

Tennessee's 95 Magic Mixes: Second Helping

Sawdust Salad

2 small boxes Jello, any flavor
4 bananas, diced
1 large can crushed pineapple, drained reserving 1 cup
2 tablespoons flour
¾ cup sugar

2 eggs
2 packages Dream Whip
1 (3-ounce) package cream cheese
½ pound cheese, grated

Mix Jello as per directions on box; add diced bananas and drained pineapple. In double boiler, cook pineapple juice, flour, sugar, and eggs until thick. Cool completely and pour over Jello mixture. Stir prepared Dream Whip and cream cheese together and spread on top of sugar and egg mixture. Top with grated cheese and chill.

Cookin' & Quiltin'

Orange Party Salad

1 small can crushed pineapple, drained
1 can mandarin oranges, drained
2 cups liquid from fruit
1 (6-ounce) package orange Jello

2 tablespoons sugar
1 (3-ounce) package cream cheese
15 large marshmallows
½ pint heavy cream, whipped

Drain pineapple and orange sections. Add enough water to make 2 cups. Heat to boiling and pour over gelatin. Cool and add pineapple and orange sections. Place in refrigerator and when it is completely cold add whipping cream. Dissolve sugar in this. Add cream cheese and marshmallows to hot mixture. Pour in mold, refrigerate.

Note: I always double this recipe because it is so good it goes fast.

Parties & Pleasures

Congealed Spiced Peach Salad

1 (16-ounce) can sliced peaches
¼ cup vinegar
½ cup sugar
12 whole cloves
⅛ teaspoon cinnamon
1 (3-ounce) package orange
  gelatin
¾ cup cold water

Drain peaches, saving 1 cup syrup. Chop peaches coarsely. Bring syrup, vinegar, sugar and spices to a boil and simmer for 10 minutes. Strain syrup and discard cloves. Dissolve gelatin in hot syrup. Add cold water and peaches. Chill until slightly thickened. Pour into mold or 9 × 9 dish.

Recipes from Miss Daisy's

Cinnamon Mold

I love this salad. It is so good with ham.

2 (3-ounce) packages lemon
  gelatin
½ cup red cinnamon candies
3 cups boiling water
2 cups unsweetened applesauce
1 tablespoon lemon juice
Dash salt
½ cup broken pecans
2 (3-ounce) packages cream
  cheese
¼ cup milk
2 tablespoons mayonnaise

Dissolve gelatin and candies in boiling water. Add applesauce, lemon juice and salt. Chill until partially set. Add pecans. Pour into 8-inch dish. Cream together cream cheese, milk and mayonnaise and top gelatin mixture. Either chill until set and slice with the two layers or take a silver knife and make a marble effect with the gelatin and creamed mixtures. Chill until firm and serve on lettuce leaf.

. . . and garnish with Memories

Roquefort Cheese Salad-Dessert

3 envelopes unflavored gelatin
2 cups cold water
1 cup crumbled Roquefort
  cheese
1 cup cottage cheese
1 (3-ounce) package cream
  cheese, softened

1 cup heavy cream, whipped
3 cups mandarin orange sections
1 cup whole fresh strawberries
  or fruit in season
Watercress or mint leaves

Sprinkle gelatin over cold water and stir in to soften. Heat to dissolve gelatin, stirring constantly. Cool. Beat Roquefort cheese, cottage cheese, and cream cheese until smooth. Gradually add gelatin mixture, beating until smooth. Chill until slightly thickened. Fold in whipped cream and turn into a greased 9-inch ring mold with about a 6-cup capacity. Chill until set. Unmold onto platter and fill center with orange sections. Garnish with strawberries or fruit in season and decorate with watercress or mint leaves. Preparation time: 30 minutes plus 3 hours chilling time. Yield: 8 servings.

Note: This is colorful and refreshing, but rich. I prefer it for dessert, as it is a pleasing combination of cheese and fruit.

Nashville Seasons

Paper Cup Frozen Salad

2 cups sour cream
2 tablespoons lemon juice
½ cup sugar
1 (8½-ounce) can crushed
  pineapple, drained

1 banana
½ cup pecans
1 can bing cherries pitted
⅛ teaspoon salt

Mix all together. Pour into paper cups almost full. Freeze. Store in plastic bags after frozen and use as needed.

Palate Pleasers

Eggnog Ring

1 (3-ounce) package lemon
flavor Jello
2 cups boiling water
¼ cup cold water
¼ teaspoon rum extract
(optional)
¾ cup canned eggnog
1 (8-ounce) can pear halves or ½
cup seeded halved grapes

1 (11-ounce) can mandarin
orange sections
1 (3-ounce) package cherry or
raspberry flavor Jello
Maraschino cherries (optional)
1½ cups pecans (optional)

Dissolve lemon gelatin in 1 cup boiling water. Add ¼ cup cold water and extract. Measure ¾ cup gelatin and add eggnog. Pour into a 6-cup ring mold. Chill until set but not firm, about 25 minutes.

Drain fruits, measuring syrup. Add water to syrup to make ¾ cup. Dice pears. Dissolve cherry gelatin in 1 cup boiling water. Add measured liquid and the remaining lemon gelatin. Chill until thick. Add pears and spoon into mold over eggnog. Arrange oranges in gelatin near edge of mold, pressing down lightly. Chill until firm, about 4 hours. Unmold* and garnish with cherries, if desired. For an attractive addition, fill center with pecans. Makes 5½ cups or 10 servings.

*To unmold, dip mold just to the rim in warm water. Loosen gelatin at edge of mold with fingertips. Shake gently. Place moistened plate over mold and invert. Lift off mold.

Elvis Fans Cookbook II

Frozen Cucumber Stuffing

2 cucumbers, peeled
1 tablespoon lemon juice
1 teaspoon Worcestershire sauce
¾ teaspoon salt

1 tablespoon chopped onion
½ teaspoon white pepper
½ cup mayonnaise
½ cup sour cream

Blanch cucumbers for 5 minutes in boiling water with lemon juice. Drain and finely chop. Combine with Worcestershire sauce, salt, onion, white pepper, mayonnaise, and sour cream. Freeze, stirring occasionally. Fill tomatoes with cucumber mixture and garnish with mayonnaise and finely chopped parsley. Preparation time: 15 minutes plus 2 hours freezing time. Yield: 6 servings.

Nashville Seasons

Fire and Ice Tomatoes

¾ cup vinegar
¼ cup cold water
1½ teaspoons mustard seed
1½ teaspoons celery salt
½ teaspoon salt
4½ teaspoons sugar

⅛ teaspoon red pepper
⅛ teaspoon black pepper
6 large tomatoes, cut in quarters
1 onion, cut in slices and
    separated
1 bell pepper, cut in strips

Combine vinegar, water, and seasonings. Boil one minute. Pour over vegetables and chill several hours. Will keep 2 to 3 days.

The James K. Polk Cookbook

Far East Spinach Salad

DRESSING:

1 cup vegetable oil
¼ cup vinegar
⅓ cup catsup

1 tablespoon sugar
1 medium onion, grated
Salt to taste

SALAD:

1 pound fresh spinach, washed, dried and chilled
¾ pound fresh bean sprouts, rinsed, dried and chilled or 1 (18-ounce) can bean sprouts, drained
1 (8-ounce) can water chestnuts, sliced

2 hard-boiled eggs, chopped
6–8 slices bacon, cooked and crumbled
1 (11-ounce) can mandarin oranges (optional)

Mix dressing ingredients thoroughly and chill. Toss spinach lightly with bean sprouts, water chestnuts, eggs, bacon and oranges, if desired. Just before serving, toss with dressing. Yield; 6–8 servings.

Dinner on the Diner

Molded Spinach Salad

1 package lemon Jello
1¾ cups water
1½ tablespoons vinegar
½ cup real mayonnaise
¼ teaspoon salt

⅓ cup chopped celery
1 pound minced onion
1 cup chopped frozen spinach, thawed and drained
¾ cup cottage cheese

Dissolve Jello in ¾ cup boiling water; add 1 cup cold water, vinegar, mayonnaise and salt. Place in freezer tray and chill until firm about 1 inch around sides of tray. Put into bowl and beat until fluffy. Add remaining ingredients, place in 1-quart mold and chill until firm.

Grand Tour Collection

Marinated Vegetable Salad

2 tablespoons wine vinegar
¾ cup sugar
1 teaspoon salt
½ teaspoon pepper
⅓ cup oil
⅔ cup cider vinegar

Dash of garlic salt
1 cup squash, sliced
1 cup carrots, sliced
1 cup broccoli, sliced
1 cup cauliflower, sliced
1 cup tomatoes (cherry), sliced

Mix together the first seven ingredients and pour over fresh vegetables. Refrigerate overnight. Pour off marinade and serve vegetables. Serves 10 to 12.

St. Paul Cooks

Kraut and Apple Salad

1 quart chopped kraut, drained
1 large apple, chopped
1 cup celery, chopped
1 cup onion, chopped

1 cup sweet pepper, chopped (1 green and 1 red)
1 cup sugar
½ cup vinegar

Combine all ingredients and mix well. Let set at least 4 hours. Keeps well.

The Apple Barn Cookbook

Kraut Salad

1 cup sugar
½ cup vinegar
1 green pepper, chopped
1 small can chopped pimientos

1 cup chopped celery
1 large onion, chopped
1 large can sauerkraut

Boil sugar and vinegar until sugar dissolves. Pour over remaining ingredients and bring to boil again. Cool and refrigerate overnight. One carrot may be shredded and added for color. Serves 6-8.

Our Favorite Recipes

Layered Salad Supreme

3 cups mayonnaise
1 cup sour cream
2 teaspoons seasoned salt
1 teaspoon garlic powder
2 quarts chopped lettuce
3 cups chopped green pepper
1¼ quarts shredded carrots
1¼ quarts sliced cauliflower
1 quart chopped cucumber

1 quart sliced celery
3 cups sliced radishes
3½ cups chopped zucchini
2⅔ cups sliced red onion
1 pound bacon, cooked and
   chopped
6 hard-cooked eggs, chopped
1 cup parsley, minced
6 cherry tomatoes

Combine mayonnaise, sour cream, salt, and garlic powder. In 2-gallon punch bowl, layer and pack: lettuce, green pepper, carrots, cauliflower, 2 cups dressing, cucumber, celery, radishes, zucchini, onion, and remaining 2 cups dressing. Cover; refrigerate a few hours. At serving time, sprinkle bacon around edge and fill center with eggs. Garnish with parsley and tomatoes. Makes 2 gallons.

Koinonia Cooking

Avocado and Grapefruit Salad

2 grapefruit   Lemon juice
2 avocados

Peel grapefruit. Divide into sections, being careful not to break them. Peel avocados. Cut into slices lengthwise. Sprinkle avocado slices with lemon juice to prevent discoloration. Alternate grapefruit sections and avocado slices on lettuce-lined plates. Serve with Poppy Seed Dressing. Makes 4 servings.

POPPY SEED DRESSING:

Very good on fruit salad and especially good on Avocado and Grapefruit Salad.

¾ cup sugar   1 tablespoon onion juice
1 teaspoon dry mustard   ½ cup honey
1 teaspoon salt   1 cup cooking oil
⅓ cup cider vinegar   1½ tablespoons poppy seed

Combine sugar, mustard, salt, vinegar, onion juice and honey in medium bowl. Using mixer or rotary beater, gradually beat in oil until mixture is thick and smooth. Fold in poppy seed. Store in refrigerator until ready to use. Makes about 2 cups.

Minnie Pearl Cooks

Microwave Hot Potato Salad

4 slices bacon
2 small white onions, chopped
1 (10½-ounce) can cream of
  celery soup
2 tablespoons chicken broth
2 tablespoons white vinegar
½ teaspoon salt

¼ teaspoon pepper
½ teaspoon sugar
¼ teaspoon celery seed
4 medium potatoes, baked,
  peeled and diced
Parsley for garnish

Cook bacon; cool and crumble. Save 2 tablespoons bacon grease; add onions to it and cook 2 minutes on High or until transparent. Add soup, broth, vinegar, salt, pepper, sugar, and celery seed. Cook on High 2 minutes. Stir; cook on High 2 more minutes. Add potatoes and bacon. Cook on High for 30 seconds. Stir; cook 30 seconds more. Sprinkle with parsley. Serves 4.

Maury County Cookbook

Macaroni Salad
This will make you forget potato salad.

8 ounces macaroni
¾ cup Kraft Italian low calorie
  dressing
¾ cup chopped carrots
1 cup chopped celery
¼ cup chopped onion

¼–½ cup chopped green pepper
½ cup cubed or grated cheese
1 (8-ounce) carton sour cream
Celery seed
Seasoned salt
Pepper

Cook macaroni according to package directions. Drain and marinate at least overnight in Italian dressing. Add vegetables and cheese. Mix with sour cream and seasonings to taste. Refrigerate. Keeps well up to week or 10 days. Flavor improves with age.

Sam Houston Schoolhouse Cookbook

Pasta Salad

DRESSING:

½ cup red wine vinegar
2 teaspoons Dijon mustard
Salt and freshly ground pepper
 to taste
1½ cups olive oil

1–2 teaspoons dried dill (or 1
 tablespoon chopped fresh dill)
2 teaspoons dried basil
½ cup fresh chopped parsley

Whisk first four dressing ingredients together. Add dill, basil, and parsley. Mix well. Toss gently with cooked pasta. Add vegetables and toss to coat well.

SALAD:

1 recipe cooked fettuccini
½ pound fresh mushrooms,
 sliced thin
1 head broccoli flowerets,
 steamed 3 minutes then rinsed
 in cold water

4–5 green onions, sliced
1 small jar stuffed green olives,
 halved
1 pint cherry tomatoes, halved
½ pound Parmesan cheese,
 freshly grated

Chill salad, covered, for at least 2 hours. Serve on bed of Bibb lettuce with cherry tomatoes for garnish. Sprinkle cheese on top. Serve at room temperature. Yield: 8–10 servings.

Dinner on the Diner

Quick Ham Salad

2 (6¾-ounce) cans Hormel
 chunk ham
4 tablespoons sweet pickle relish
2 tablespoons vinegar

2 tablespoons mayonnaise (or
 just enough to hold mixture
 together)
Generous dash of McCormick
 lemon & pepper seasoning

Flake ham with form and add all other ingredients, and mix well. Refrigerate until ready to use. I use this ham salad for sandwiches, and as an appetizer, spread on crackers. It can also be served on lettuce, as a salad, with crackers.

Gatlinburg Recipe Collection

Different Chicken Salad

½ pound vermicelli, cooked al dente and drained
⅓ cup garlic salad dressing
Salt, to taste
3 cups cubed cooked chicken
1 (9-ounce) package frozen artichoke hearts, cooked according to directions
1 (2.2-ounce) can sliced black olives
1 tablespoon grated onion
1 cup homemade mayonnaise
4 tablespoons snipped parsley
½ cup sliced green onions
Cherry tomatoes for garnish
Avocado slices for garnish

Put warm pasta in bowl and toss well with dressing. Let cool and refrigerate several hours or overnight. When ready to serve, add chicken, artichokes and black olives to pasta. Toss this mixture gently with mayonnaise. Serve topped with parsley and green onions. Garnish with cherry tomatoes and avocado slices that have been marinated in small amount of garlic salad dressing.

Serves 6–8.

GARLIC SALAD DRESSING:

¼ cup wine vinegar
2 teaspoons Dijon mustard
4 cloves garlic, split
1 teaspoon paprika
Salt
Ground pepper
1 cup olive oil

Combine all ingredients except olive oil. Add oil slowly while whisking. This must be done at least one day ahead of time. Yields 1¼ cups.

Well Seasoned

Palace Crabmeat Salad

2 tablespoons finely chopped
  stuffed olives
1 tablespoon finely chopped
  green pepper
1 tablespoon finely chopped
  onion
1 tablespoon chili sauce
2 tablespoons cream

½ cup mayonnaise
1 (9-ounce) packages frozen
  artichoke hearts
6 tablespoons French dressing
2 (6-ounce) packages frozen
  crabmeat
1 head lettuce
2 large tomatoes

Combine first 6 ingredients, blend well, refrigerate. Cook artichokes, drain, and marinate in 3 tablespoons French dressing. Refrigerate. Drain crabmeat and marinate in 3 tablespoons French dressing; refrigerate. Arrange lettuce on platter, place crabmeat in center. Place tomato wedges and artichokes around crabmeat, spoon dressing over the platter. Garnish with parsley and radish roses. Yield: 8 servings.

Woman's Exchange Cookbook I

Roquefort Ice

¼ pound Roquefort cheese
½ pint heavy cream, whipped

Salt and pepper

Mash cheese and mix well with whipped cream. Season to taste with salt and pepper. Freeze in refrigerator tray. Serve with artichoke hearts and French Dressing on lettuce with poppy seed sprinkled lightly over the top. Serves 6.

The Memphis Cookbook

Dressing for Spinach or Lettuce Salad

½ cup salad oil
¼ cup wine vinegar (red or
  white)
1½ teaspoons sugar
2 teaspoons dry mustard
1 teaspoon salt
½ teaspoon paprika

1 tablespoon chives
1 teaspoon parsley
1 tablespoon grated onion
Freshly ground or cracked
  pepper
1 ice cube

Combine all ingredients in a jar. Shake well to blend. This is good on any mixed green salad with hard-boiled eggs, bacon and sliced fresh mushrooms. Makes about 1 cup for 8 individual salads.

Southern Secrets

Honey Dijon Salad Dressing

½ cup mayonnaise
1 tablespoon Dijon mustard
1 tablespoon honey
1 tablespoon vinegar

Horseradish to taste (optional)
Dash of Tabasco
Dash of paprika

Mix ingredients together and refrigerate.

St. Paul Cooks

Daddy's Favorite Slaw

Daddy complimented my cooking. I made some awful messes when I first started cooking but he always found something good to say about my efforts. He said my slaw was his very favorite.

1 medium head cabbage
1 medium onion, diced
2 medium cucumbers
1 cup grated Cheddar cheese
2 tomatoes, chopped

2 teaspoons salt
1 teaspoon black pepper
Mayonnaise
1 cup cheese crackers

Shred cabbage, add diced onion, cucumbers, and grated cheese. Chill until serving time. Add chopped tomatoes, salt and pepper to taste and just enough mayonnaise to hold mixture together. At the last minute, toss in cheese crackers which have been broken into bite-size pieces. Serve immediately.

... and garnish with Memories

Bread and Breakfast

Quilting is one of the many "old time" crafts still practiced and enjoyed in Tennessee.

Easy Breakfast Bake

½ pound (1 cup) pork sausage
1 teaspoon salt
2¼ cups water
¾ cup quick grits
2 tablespoons butter or margarine

2 tablespoons all-purpose flour
¼ teaspoon black pepper
1 cup milk
½ cup grated Cheddar cheese
4 eggs

Preheat oven to 325°. Brown and crumble sausage. Drain off excess fat and set aside.

Bring salted water to a boil and stir in grits. Cover and reduce heat to low. Continue cooking for 5 minutes, stirring occasionally. Melt butter or margarine and stir in flour, black pepper and milk. Cook, stirring to thicken. Add cheese, stirring until blended. Add sausage and ½ of cheese sauce to cooked grits. Pour into lightly greased casserole. Make 4 indentions into grits mixture with the back of a large spoon. Break one egg into each indention. Bake at 325° for 13–18 minutes, depending on desired doneness of eggs. Serve with remaining heated sauce. Serves 4.

Kiss My Grits

Glazed Bacon Strips
You'll get raves!

1 pound bacon, (slices cut in half)

1 (16-ounce) box brown sugar (enough to coat bacon well)

Roll each slice of bacon in brown sugar covering both sides. Place on broiler pan or rack. Bake at 325° for 15 to 30 minutes. Keep checking until bacon is browned and fat cooked from it. Place cooked bacon on foil to cool. It will crisp as it cools. Serve at room temperature. This can be made early in the day or the day before and stored covered in refrigerator until ready to use. Serve on a silver tray. Note: I use Oscar Mayer bacon. Yield: 30 or more pieces.

Flaunting Our Finest

Million Dollar Eggs

50 eggs	2 sticks butter
Homemade mayonnaise	½ cup flour
Salt	4–5 (13-ounce) cans evaporated
White pepper	milk
Worcestershire sauce	Salt, pepper, and sherry to taste
8 ounces black caviar	Parmesan cheese
1 pound grated medium	
Cheddar cheese	

Boil eggs and stuff halves with yolks, mayonnaise, salt, white pepper, and Worcestershire sauce. Do not make stuffing too firm. Line bottoms of 2 Pyrex 9 × 13-inch casseroles with stuffed eggs. Top with caviar and grated cheese. Pour over eggs a cream sauce made with 1½ sticks butter (reserve some butter to pour around edges of casseroles before cooking), flour, evaporated milk, salt, pepper, and sherry. Top with Parmesan cheese and bake 30 minutes at 350°. Serves 40 or more.

Can be made the day before and also can be halved.

The James K. Polk Cookbook

Scalloped Eggs Creole

4 cups cubed bread (½-inch squares)	1 can tomato sauce
8 tablespoons butter or more	1 tablespoon parsley
2 heaping tablespoons chopped onion	1 teaspoon celery salt
2 heaping tablespoons green pepper, chopped	2 cups cream sauce (medium)
	12 large eggs, hard boiled

Sauté bread squares in butter until light brown. For creole sauce: Brown lightly onions and pepper in heavy skillet, add tomato sauce, let simmer slightly, add parsley and celery salt. Use large casserole and put in layers: Bread squares, cream sauce, sliced eggs, creole sauce. Repeat layers, ending with bread squares on top. The consistency of the ingredients should not be too thick. If so, add a little tomato juice or sauce. If too thin, add more bread crumbs. Bake in 350° oven 30 minutes. Serves 8.

This is delicious; with a green salad makes a very adequate meal.

Woman's Exchange Cookbook I

"Cheese Sandwich" Souffle

A cheese souffle that doesn't fall, that can be either a main dish or a side dish on a big buffet with ham, that can be made way ahead of time, and a souffle that even the children will eat, is what we are all looking for.

This one is actually a cheese casserole. Made by spreading bread slices with soft butter and cheese, cubing them, and putting them in a casserole with eggs and milk, this souffle mellows and seasons before baking. The children call it cheese sandwich souffle because under all the puffy glamor, there is the familiar taste of their favorite grilled cheese sandwich. If you are having it for supper, have a molded fruit salad with it.

¼ pound butter
½ pound Cheddar cheese, grated
9 slices regular bread
2 eggs

2 cups milk
Salt and pepper
Dash of Worcestershire

Cream together butter and cheese. Take regular bread and decrust. (I use Pepperidge Farm type bread, but you don't have to.) Spread each slice with butter and cheese and then cut in cubes. Place in baking dish lightly. Beat well eggs and milk. Add salt, pepper, and Worcestershire. Pour lightly into baking dish. Turn bread so that it is all wet.

The baking dish may be a cast iron casserole. It may set overnight or a few hours in the refrigerator. Let get to room temperature before baking, and fluff it up again. Bake at 350 for 1 hour. Don't let it burn.

Chattanooga Cook Book

Cream Cheese Grits

1 cup grits
3 cups water

Salt

Cook until soupy and add:

1 (8-ounce) package cream
   cheese

1 stick butter
Grated Cheddar cheese

In a cup measure two eggs with enough milk to make a full cup. Beat eggs and milk together and add to first mixture. Bake at 350° for 30 minutes. Top with grated Cheddar cheese and bake 10 more minutes.

The Sevier County Cookbook

Cheese Grits

4 cups boiling water
1 teaspoon salt

1 cup grits, washed
1 cup cheese, grated

Bring water and salt to a boil. When water has boiled, stir in grits and cook slowly for 30 minutes. Then add cheese, blending thoroughly.

Cracker Barrel Old Country Stores:
Old Timey Recipes & Proverbs to Live By

Garlic Cheese Grits

1 cup quick-cooking grits
1 roll garlic cheese
1 stick butter

2 eggs, beaten
¾ cup milk

Cook grits as package directs. Add cheese and butter. Cool. Combine eggs and milk. Put grits in 2-quart buttered casserole and pour egg-milk mixture over grits. Bake uncovered for 1 hour in 375° oven. Can be made ahead. Note: Egg-milk mixture can be stirred into the cooled grits, if desired, and top dusted with paprika. Serves 8.

Party Potpourri

Garlic Cheese Grits

2 cups water
1 cup quick grits
½ teaspoon salt
8 ounces garlic cheese
½ cup butter or margarine

Tabasco sauce (a dash)
2 egg yolks, beaten
2 egg whites, stiffly beaten
Salt and pepper to taste
Worcestershire sauce (to taste)

Preheat oven to 350°. Bring salted water to a boil and stir in grits, slowly. Cook for 2 minutes. Remove from heat and add cheese (cut into 6–8 pieces) and butter or margarine. Place back on medium heat and continue to cook until cheese is completely melted. Remove from heat and add egg yolks, salt and pepper to taste. Mix thoroughly, then add Tabasco sauce and Worcestershire sauce, mixing well. Fold in stiff egg whites and then pour into greased casserole. Bake at 350° for 30 minutes (or until browned). Serves 6.

Kiss My Grits

Saw Mill Gravy

1 pound sausage
2 tablespoons of flour or more
(depends on how much you
want to make)

Milk
Salt and pepper to taste

Make sausage into patties and fry in moderately hot skillet until brown and cooked done. Put sausage patties on paper towel to drain grease. Use about ½ of the grease in skillet to make gravy. Add flour and brown flour in grease stirring constantly. Add about 1½ cups of milk and enough water to make gravy as thin as you like. Break up about 4 of the cooked sausage patties and crumble in the gravy. Salt and pepper to taste. Serve over hot biscuits.

This gravy gets its name from the saw mill camps that were in the Smoky Mountain area years ago. Saw mill gravy was also made from bacon the same way as from sausage in the camps. Gravy was always served for breakfast and sometimes other meals.

Gatlinburg Recipe Collection

Country Ham and Red-Eye Gravy

Country ham is usually sliced about ¼-inch thick. Trim off outside skin, leaving some of the fat. Put about 2 teaspoons of corn oil in an iron skillet, enough to grease bottom of pan. Heat skillet and fry ham until slightly brown on both sides (ham does not take long to cook). Remove ham to warm platter, and make red-eye gravy by adding ¼ to ½ cup of water to hot skillet, let sizzle, and pour over ham. (Can add a small amount of ready-to-drink coffee to gravy, if desired). Biscuits always go well with country ham, and when I was a kid I liked to sop my biscuits in red-eye gravy. I am not a kid anymore but, I still like to sop a biscuit in red-eye gravy. I also like to grill country ham on a charcoal or gas grill. It's quick and easy to do for a party. There's no red-eye gravy when you grill country ham, but it's very good.

Gatlinburg Recipe Collection

Beer Biscuits

4 cups Bisquick mix
2 tablespoons sugar
¼ cup oil

1 (12-ounce) can Budweiser beer
(room temperature)

In bowl combine Bisquick mix and sugar; add ¼ cup oil, and beer, and mix well. Warm well-greased muffin pans in oven. Fill muffin pans ½ to ⅔ full of mixture. Bake in 400° oven about 15 minutes until golden brown.

I had this recipe a long time before I tried to make it. I didn't want to buy the beer. One day a Budweiser beer truck was on the road passing my house, and a carton of beer slid out when a back door on the truck came open accidentally. The driver didn't know he lost the beer and he didn't come back for it, so I got the beer and decided to make the beer biscuits. I used up the beer a long time ago and have had to buy some but I hope that another Budweiser truck comes my way again, and manages to lose some more beer, for my beer biscuits.

Gatlinburg Recipe Collection

Momma Rogers' Melt in Your Mouth Butter Biscuits

2 sticks real butter, softened
2 cups self-rising flour
8 ounces sour cream

Tiny cup muffin tin or tartlet pan

Mix first two ingredients, then add 8 ounces sour cream. Drop by spoon into muffin tin. Bake at 450° for 8 to 10 minutes. Do not grease muffin pan. Makes about 50 small bite-size biscuits.

This is the easiest ever to prepare! They are wonderful!

St. Paul Cooks

Lucy's Biscuits

In 1977 my husband was in the military, and we were stationed overseas. He wrote home to Lucy Fitzhugh at Lucy's Cafe on the square in Dover, Tennessee, and requested her recipe for biscuits. He thought they were the best in the world, and he wanted to give the recipe to the cook on his ship. In return my husband sent her a color aerial photo of the submarine squadron at Polaris Point, Guam. She displayed the photo and his letter requesting her biscuit recipe in the cafe until it closed. They are the best biscuits in the world. I have included my own version.

5 cups self-rising flour
½ teaspoon soda
1 cup lard

2 cups buttermilk
1 package yeast
¼ cup warm water

Dissolve yeast in warm water and set aside. In large bowl, sift together 4 cups flour and baking soda. Cut in lard until it looks like coarse crumbs. Mix together remaining 1 cup flour with the buttermilk; add yeast mixture. Add buttermilk and yeast mixture to the flour and mix well. Turn out onto lightly floured surface and knead. Place in greased bowl, covered, in refrigerator. Biscuits are ready to bake at any time. When ready to bake, roll and cut as many as needed. Bake in a 425° oven for about 15 minutes. Yield: approximately 3 dozen biscuits.

The Original Tennessee Homecoming Cookbook

Low-Sodium Biscuits

2 cups sifted all-purpose plain
  flour
2 teaspoons sugar
4½ teaspoons low-sodium
  baking powder

⅓ cup unsalted shortening
¾ cup of buttermilk

Measure flour. Sift with sugar and baking powder. Cut in shortening until mixture looks like meal. Stir in buttermilk. Knead 25 times; roll out ½-inch thick. Cut with 2-inch cutter and place biscuits on ungreased baking sheet. Bake in a 450° oven for 10–12 minutes or until golden brown. Yield: Sixteen 2-inch biscuits. Serving: 1 biscuit-10 milligrams sodium, 95 calories.

Change of Seasons

Potato Biscuits

½ cup milk
4 tablespoons shortening
¼ cup sugar
½ cup hot riced potatoes

¾ teaspoon salt
1 cake yeast, softened in ¼ cup
  lukewarm water
2½ cups all-purpose flour

Scald milk. Cool to lukewarm. Stir in shortening, sugar, potatoes, salt, yeast and ½ cup flour. Cover. Let rise until light. Add 2 cups flour, cover and let rise again.

Turn onto floured board, pat and roll ¼-inch thick. Shape in any way you prefer. Let rise. Bake at 425° for 12–20 minutes, according to size of biscuits. Makes about 18.

Rich Potato Biscuits: After adding yeast, add 1 egg (yolk and white beaten separately).

Our Favorite Recipes

Salty Dogs
Crisp Onion Biscuits

2 cups plain flour
1 teaspoon soda
½ teaspoon salt
1 package onion soup mix (dry)

½ cup Crisco
¼ cup apple cider vinegar
½ cup sweet milk
Caraway seeds and coarse salt

Combine flour, soda, salt and dry onion soup mix. Work in ½ cup Crisco with fingers. Add vinegar to sweet milk and combine all at once with dry ingredients. Shape dough into small fingers and roll lightly in caraway seeds and salt. Bake in slow 275° oven until brown and crisp.

Kountry Kooking

Spicy Apple Pancakes with Cider Sauce

2 cups biscuit baking mix
½ teaspoon cinnamon
1 egg

1⅓ cups milk
¾ cup grated apple (about 2
    medium apples)

Beat baking mix, cinnamon, egg and milk with rotary beater until smooth. Stir in apples. Grease griddle if necessary and pour batter by ¼-cup measure onto hot griddle. Bake until bubbles appear, turn and bake other side until golden brown. Serve with warm cider sauce; if desired, top with sour cream. Yield: 18 (4-inch) pancakes.

CIDER SAUCE:
1 cup sugar
2 tablespoons cornstarch
¼ teaspoon nutmeg

2 cups apple cider
2 tablespoons lemon juice
¼ cup butter or margarine

In saucepan, mix sugar, cornstarch, cinnamon and nutmeg; stir in cider and lemon juice. Cook over medium heat, stirring constantly, until mixture thickens and boils. Boil and stir for 1 minute. Remove from heat and stir in butter. Yield: about 2½ cups.

Tennessee's 95 Magic Mixes: Second Helping

Cranberry Coffee Cake

½ cup butter or margarine, softened
1 cup sugar
2 eggs
2 cups all-purpose flour, sifted before measuring
1 teaspoon baking powder
1 teaspoon baking soda
½ teaspoon salt
1 cup sour cream
1 teaspoon almond extract
1 (16-ounce) can whole cranberry sauce
½ cup chopped pecans

Preheat oven to 350°. Cream butter and sugar together until light and fluffy. Add eggs, one at a time, beating thoroughly after each. Combine flour, baking powder, baking soda and salt. Add flour mixture to creamed mixture alternately with sour cream, beating well after each addition. Add almond extract and mix well.

Spoon a third of mixture into a greased and floured 10-inch tube pan. Spread a third of cranberry sauce over batter. Repeat layers twice more, ending with cranberry sauce. Sprinkle pecans over top. Bake for 1 hour or until cake tests done. Let cool 5 minutes before removing from pan.

GLAZE:

¾ cup sifted powdered sugar
½ teaspoon almond extract
2 tablespoons warm water

Combine glaze ingredients and mix well. Drizzle over top of coffee cake after removing from pan. Yield: 1 cake.

Dinner on the Diner

72

Bran Muffins by the Pail Full

4 cups All Bran
2 cups 100% Bran
1 teaspoon salt
2 cups boiling water
1 quart buttermilk

3 cups sugar
1 cup shortening
4 eggs
5 cups pre-sifted flour
5 teaspoons soda

Combine Brans and salt. Stir in water and then buttermilk. Cool to lukewarm. Cream sugar and shortening; add eggs, one at a time, beating well after each addition. Stir into Bran mixture. Combine flour and soda. Add to Bran mixture and stir to just dampen dry ingredients. Store in refrigerator until ready to use.

TO BAKE: Fill greased muffin tins ⅔ full and bake 20–25 minutes, in pre-heated 375° oven. If desired, add dates, raisins or blueberries just before baking. Makes 72 muffins.

Smoky Mountain Magic

Whole Wheat Muffins
Good sweet muffin

2 cups whole wheat flour
¼ cup sugar
1 teaspoon salt
3 teaspoons baking powder

1 cup milk
1 egg
3 tablespoons butter or
    margarine, melted

Mix dry ingredients. Add milk, beaten egg, and melted butter. Beat well. Pour into greased muffin tins. Bake 20 to 25 minutes at 375°. Yield: 6 muffins.

Encore! Nashville

Nashville is the political capital of Tennessee, and the country music capital of the world. Called Music City USA, it is the home of the famous Grand Ole Opry, which is nothing less than an American institution.

Sedberry Inn Pineapple Muffins
Everyone will want the recipe.

¾ cup butter
1½ cups sugar
3 eggs, beaten
3 cups flour

3 teaspoons baking powder
1 (16-ounce) can crushed
   pineapple
2 tablespoons orange extract

Cream butter and sugar (do not overbeat). Add beaten eggs and beat lightly. Add dry ingredients, then pineapple and flavoring, mixing only until blended. Bake in greased muffin tins at 350° for about 20 minutes. Do not allow muffins to brown. Ice with the following icing while the muffins are still hot.

ICING:
2 tablespoons milk
2 tablespoons butter

2 cups powdered sugar
2 tablespoons orange extract

In a saucepan, heat the milk and butter, but do not boil. Add the powdered sugar and extract; mix well. Yield: 3 dozen.

Out of this World

Pumpkin Bread

3 cups sugar
1 cup salad oil
4 eggs, beaten
1 (1-pound) can pumpkin
3½ cups all-purpose flour
2 teaspoons soda
1 teaspoon salt

2 teaspoons baking powder
1 teaspoon nutmeg
1 teaspoon allspice
1 teaspoon cinnamon
½ teaspoon cloves
⅔ cup water

Cream sugar and oil together. Add eggs and pumpkin and mix well. Sift together the dry ingredients. Add dry ingredients alternately with water. Pour into 2 well-greased and floured 9 × 5-inch loaf pans. Bake at 350° for 1 to 1½ hours (or until test done). Let stand 10 minutes, then remove from pans to cool. Makes 2 loaves:

Great with Sunday brunch or as a dessert served with fruit or ice cream!

A Man's Taste

Smoky Mountain Log Cabin Bread

1 cup raisins
2 cups boiling water
3 tablespoons honey
3 tablespoons molasses
¼ cup oil
1 teaspoon salt

1 tablespoon dry yeast
¼ cup lukewarm water
1 egg
3 cups unbleached flour
2 cups whole wheat flour

Boil raisins in water for 20 minutes. Drain raisins and put raisin water into a large bowl with honey, molasses, oil and salt. Mix until lukewarm and add yeast dissolved in lukewarm water. Beat in egg and gradually add about 3 cups unbleached flour and 2 cups whole wheat flour. Beat until dough gets real sticky. Then add the raisins and enough more flour until you can handle the bread. Grease it well and let rise for 1 hour. Punch it down and knead until smooth. Shape into loaves. Let rise till double in size and bake in 325° oven for 50 minutes. Wrap in cloth to keep moist. Delightful toasted.

Tennessee Homecoming: Famous Parties, People & Places

Onion-Cheese Supper Bread

½ cup chopped onions
1 tablespoon fat
1 beaten egg
½ cup milk

1½ cups biscuit mix
1 cup grated sharp American
  cheese
1 tablespoon poppy seed

Cook onion in fat until tender and light brown. Combine egg and milk. Add to biscuit mix and stir only until the dry ingredients are just moistened. Add onion and half of the grated cheese. Spread dough in greased 8 inch round baking dish. Sprinkle top with remaining cheese and poppy seed. Drizzle melted butter over all. Bake 20–25 minutes at 400°. Serve hot with cold meat slices and tossed salad.

Smoky Mountain Magic

Monkey Bread

1 cup butter, no substitutions,
  divided
1 cup milk
1 package dry yeast
⅓ cup warm water

2 eggs
½ cup sugar
½ teaspoon salt
3 cups flour

Melt half of the butter in a saucepan. Add milk and scald. Remove from heat and cool. Dissolve yeast in warm water and add to milk mixture. Beat together eggs, sugar and salt, and add to yeast mixture. Stir in 1½ cups flour and mix well by hand. Place in large bowl and add remaining flour. Mix well and form a ball of dough. Cover and let rise for one hour. Melt ¼ cup butter. Cut remaining ¼ cup butter into cubes and place around bottom of tube or bundt pan. Spoon bread dough into pan and pour melted butter over it. Bake at 375° for 30 minutes. Yield: 8 servings.

Upper Crust: A Slice of the South

Cream Cheese Braids

1 cup sour cream	2 packages dry yeast
½ cup sugar	½ cup warm water
1 teaspoon salt	2 eggs, beaten
½ cup melted butter	4 cups all-purpose flour

Heat sour cream over low heat; stir in sugar, salt and butter; cool to lukewarm. Sprinkle yeast over warm water in a large bowl, stirring until yeast dissolves. Add sour cream mixture, eggs and flour; mix well. Cover tightly and refrigerate overnight. The next day, divide dough into 4 equal parts. Roll out each part on a well-floured board into a 12 × 8-inch rectangle. Spread ¼ of cream cheese filling on each rectangle. Roll up jelly roll fashion, beginning at long sides. Pinch edges under. Place each roll seam side down on greased baking sheets. Slit each roll at 2-inch intervals about ⅔ of the way through dough to resemble a braid. Cover and let rise in a warm place until doubled. Bake at 375° for 12 to 15 minutes. Spread with glaze while warm. Yields 4 loaves.

CREAM CHEESE FILLING:

2 (8-ounce) packages cream cheese	1 egg, beaten
¾ cup sugar	⅛ teaspoon salt
	2 teaspoons vanilla

Combine cream cheese, sugar and salt in a small mixing bowl. Add egg and vanilla and mix well.

GLAZE:

2 cups powdered sugar	2 teaspoons vanilla
4 tablespoons milk	

Combine all ingredients in a small bowl and mix well.

Southern Secrets

Angel Rolls

1 package dry yeast
3 cups self-rising flour
1 tablespoon sugar*

½ cup Crisco
1 cup buttermilk

Dissolve yeast in 2 tablespoons warm water; set aside. Combine flour, sugar, and Crisco; blend with a pastry cutter. Combine dissolved yeast and buttermilk; add gradually to flour mixture. Mix and store in greased bowl overnight. (May be used in an hour or two.) Dough will keep in refrigerator for several days. As needed, pinch off and shape into rolls; let stand for rising 30–40 minutes. Cook about 15 minutes at 425°.

*Use 2 tablespoons sugar for a sweeter roll.

Koinonia Cooking

Ruby's Rolls
Old stand by

1 package dry yeast
¼ cup sugar
¼ cup melted shortening
¼ cup powdered milk

1 cup warm water
1 teaspoon salt
1 egg
3½–4 cups flour

Dissolve yeast in warm water for 10 minutes. Add sugar, salt, shortening to the yeast. Beat egg and add. Then add powdered milk and flour to make a soft dough.

Let rise until doubled in bulk (about 1½ hours). Roll out on floured board. Cut with biscuit cutter, brush with melted butter and fold over. Let rise for another hour and bake at 450° until brown. I call this a "never fail" recipe for yeast rolls. My two sons like these so much that one of my sons makes them himself. The original recipe came from a cook at the old Everett High School.

Sam Houston Schoolhouse Cookbook

Spinach Rolls
Sure to impress any group

4 (10-ounce) packages chopped spinach
1 bunch fresh green onions, chopped (tops, too)
4 tablespoons margarine
¼ teaspoon salt
¼ teaspoon pepper
4 tablespoons parsley
1½ tablespoons dill seed

1½–2 pounds Monterey Jack cheese, shredded
⅓ cup Parmesan cheese
6 eggs, beaten
1 (16-ounce) box filo strudel dough (found in the frozen food department)
3 sticks margarine, melted

Cook spinach till tender. Drain well. (Squeeze out water by hand.) Sauté onions in 4 tablespoons margarine just till tender. Add onions, salt, pepper, parsley, dill seed, Monterey Jack cheese, Parmesan cheese, and eggs to the drained, cooked spinach. Mix well. Divide mixture into 4 equal portions. Set aside.

Thaw filo dough according to package directions. Be careful not to let dough become too dry. Box contains 20 sheets of dough. Use 5 sheets for each spinach roll. Remove 1 sheet of dough at a time. Place on counter and brush 1 side completely with melted butter. Carefully lay a second sheet on top of first and again spread melted butter over all. Continue until 5 sheets have been prepared. Now place ¼ of the spinach mixture along the long edge. Roll up spinach in the dough, tucking in the edges as you roll. Continue with the next 5 filo sheets and spinach. Place rolls on large cookie sheet. Spread tops with melted butter. Bake at 350° for 45 minutes, until golden brown. Serve hot. Pastry will become very flaky. Wonderful!

St. Paul Cooks

Davy Crockett was a pioneer, bear hunter, and soldier who left his mark all across Tennessee. A reconstruction of his log cabin home stands in Rutherford.

Corn Bread

1¾ cups self-rising corn meal
1½ cups buttermilk (do not use milk)
¼ teaspoon soda (mix in buttermilk)

2 tablespoons hot bacon grease
¼ cup sour cream

Mix all together and stir well. Grease iron skillet and heat it before adding mixture. Bake at 450° for 25 to 30 minutes or until brown. I use pie-shaped iron skillet that browns each piece separately. (If thicker batter is desired, add a little extra meal).

Gatlinburg Recipe Collection

Mammy's Cracklin' Corn Bread

1 cup yellow corn meal
½ cup all-purpose flour
1½ teaspoons baking powder
1 egg
½ cup pea-size cracklings

1 teaspoon salt
2 teaspoons sugar
1 cup buttermilk
¼ teaspoon soda
1 tablespoon bacon fat

Heat a heavy 10-inch skillet with oven-proof handle in oven 5 to 10 minutes. While skillet heats, scoop corn meal lightly into measuring cup. Sift flour, measure and resift 3 times with corn meal and next 4 ingredients, the last time into mixing bowl. Add buttermilk, egg and cracklings, beat hard until well mixed. Remove skillet from oven, add bacon fat and tilt back-and-forth to coat inside. Pour batter into hot skillet. Bake in hot oven (450°) 25 to 30 minutes. Serve very hot.

Tennessee Treasure

Spinach Spoonbread

1 package frozen onions in
  cream sauce
1 (10-ounce) package chopped
  spinach
2 eggs, slightly beaten
1 cup sour cream

¼ teaspoon salt
1 (8-ounce) package corn muffin
  mix
½ cup (2-ounces) Swiss cheese
  or Cheddar cheese, shredded

Prepare onions according to directions on package; set aside. Cook spinach; drain well. In large mixer bowl combine all ingredients. Pour into greased 1½-quart casserole. Bake at 350° for 30–35 minutes. Serve warm.

Koinonia Cooking

Parmesan Roll-Ups

1 large loaf thin-sliced white
  bread
1 (8-ounce) jar Cheese-Whiz

1 cup melted butter
1 (8-ounce) package Parmesan
  cheese, grated

Remove crusts from each slice of bread. Flatten each piece with a rolling pin. Spread each slice thinly with Cheese-Whiz, (don't glob). Roll each piece like a crescent roll. Dip quickly in melted butter (I use tongs for this). Roll in the grated Parmesan cheese. Bake at 350° for 10 to 12 minutes until lightly brown, on un-greased cookie sheet. Freeze immediately on tray. When partially frozen, cut in halves. Store in freezer bags. To serve, reheat in 375° oven for 12 to 15 minutes. This goes from freezer to oven.

Gatlinburg Recipe Collection

Mr. Mac's Hush Puppies

John McDonald, whom everyone lovingly calls "Mr. Mac," loves to cook hush puppies at our house when we cook the fish my husband catches. This is his recipe and when he says, "a fist full of cheese," he has a mighty big fist!

2 cups corn meal
1 tablespoon baking soda
1 teaspoon baking powder
1 tablespoon salt
½ cup grated sharp cheese

1 egg
¼ cup chopped onion
1 cup buttermilk
Dash of cayenne pepper

Mix all ingredients in above order. Form mixture into small balls. Fry in deep fat until golden brown. Makes about 16 small hush puppies.

Minnie Pearl Cooks

Miss Daisy's Hot Ham Sandwich

1 thick slice homemade bread,
   white or rye
1 slice Swiss cheese

1 slice of baked ham
4 spears of asparagus
Horseradish Sauce

Preheat oven to 400°. Layer bread, cheese, ham and asparagus. Bake 10–15 minutes or until cheese is melted.

SAUCE:
1 cup mayonnaise
1 tablespoon horseradish

Mix and heat until warm. Pour over sandwich.

Miss Daisy Entertains

Bacon-Cheese Sandwich Spread

¼ cup roasted, unblanched
   almonds
2 slices bacon, cooked
1 cup American cheese, grated

1 tablespoon green onion,
   chopped
½ cup mayonnaise

Chop almonds until fine and crumble cooked bacon. Combine all ingredients and mix to spreading consistency. Spread on whole wheat bread and cut to desired size. Broil in oven until cheese begins to melt. Serve immediately.

Gazebo Gala

Honey Wheat Bread

2 cups whole wheat flour
½ teaspoon salt
1 teaspoon baking soda

2 tablespoons honey
1 cup buttermilk
1 egg, slightly beaten

In large bowl, mix flour, salt, and soda. Make a well in the center. Add honey, buttermilk, and egg. Stir just until moistened (batter will be soft). Place in greased 1-quart casserole and bake at 375° for 20 to 25 minutes. Cool before serving. Yield: 8 to 10 servings.

Flaunting Our Finest

Iced Cheese Sandwiches
Great to have in the freezer for unexpected guests

2 cups butter or margarine,
softened
4 (5-ounce) jars soft Cheddar
cheese
1 teaspoon Tabasco sauce
1 teaspoon onion powder
1½ teaspoons Worcestershire
sauce

1 teaspoon Beau Monde
seasoning
1½ teaspoons dill weed
2½ loaves thinly sliced bread,
crusts removed

Combine butter and cheese in a mixer until fluffy. Add remaining ingredients, except the bread. Spread 3 slices of bread with the mixture and stack on top of each other. Spread sides with mixture and cut into 4 squares. Spread mixture on the cut sides. Ice the remaining slices of bread as described above. Place on waxed paper and freeze. Remove to plastic bags and freeze until ready to use. Thaw and place on cookie sheet. Bake at 325° for 15 minutes or until edges are browned. Yield: 60 sandwiches.

Encore! Nashville

Mushroom Sandwiches

1 cup chopped mushroom caps,
well drained
2 tablespoons butter

¼ cup light cream
1 tablespoon flour, sifted
8 slices bread

Sauté mushrooms in butter until tender. Add cream and flour. Cook until thick. Cool. Trim crusts from bread and cut in half. Spread mushroom mixture on bread and roll, securing with a toothpick. Toast under broiler and serve immediately. Yield: 16 sandwiches. Preparation time: 15 minutes.

Nashville Seasons

Poultry and Game

The Museum of Appalacchia is considered to have the most complete collection of mountain culture found anywhere. Norris.

Chicken Puffs

2 cups cooked, cubed chicken
½ teaspoon salt
⅛ teaspoon pepper
3 ounces cream cheese, softened
2 tablespoons milk
1 tablespoon minced onion
1 tablespoon pimiento
1 (8-ounce) can Pillsbury
  Crescent Dinner Rolls

1 tablespoon butter, melted
¾ cup Parmesan cheese or
  crushed seasoned croutons
½ (10¾-ounce) can cream of
  chicken or cream of celery
  soup

Blend first 7 ingredients. Separate rolls into 4 rectangles and seal perforations. Spoon ½ cup chicken mixture into center of each rectangle. Pull up corners and seal. Brush tops with melted butter. Dip in croutons or sprinkle with Parmesan cheese. Bake at 350° on ungreased cookie sheet 20–25 minutes, or until golden brown. Heat soup, undiluted or thinned with a little milk, and spoon over top of each puff. Serves 4.

Easy to double and can be made in advance. You may substitute crabmeat, shrimp, tuna or your favorite ground beef mixture for the chicken. You may also substitute a cream sauce for the soup.

Well Seasoned

Creamed Chicken

2 sticks butter
4 tablespoons flour
½ pint whole milk
½ pint whipping cream, not
  whipped

1 medium onion, chopped
1 teaspoon salt
½ teaspoon Worcestershire sauce
½ teaspoon A-1 sauce
2 cups cooked chicken, cubed

Melt butter and add flour. Slowly add milk, stirring constantly. Add whipping cream, onion, salt, Worcestershire and A-1 sauce. Cook until thick, add chicken and heat. Delicious served over cornbread!

Rivertown Recipes

Chicken Divan

2 (10-ounce) packages frozen broccoli
2 cups cooked chicken or 3 chicken breasts, cooked and boned
1 small can pimentos
1 cup mayonnaise
1 carton sour cream
2 cans cream of chicken soup
Swiss cheese

Cook broccoli according to package directions. Line casserole with broccoli then add sliced chicken, then layer of pimento, split open. Mix mayonnaise, sour cream, and soup. Spread over all being sure broccoli is covered. Top with slices of Swiss cheese. Bake at 350°, uncovered until bubbly or about 25 minutes. Serves 6.

St. Paul Cooks

Almond Chicken Baked in Cream

1 fryer, cut up (or two chicken breasts)
Flour
1 teaspoon celery salt
1 teaspoon paprika
1 teaspoon salt
½ teaspoon curry powder
½ teaspoon oregano
½ teaspoon pepper
6 tablespoons butter, melted
Sliced almonds
1½ cups half and half cream
½ cup sour cream

Coat chicken with flour. Blend seasonings with melted butter and coat chicken. Arrange chicken in single layer in baking dish. Sprinkle evenly with sliced almonds. Pour half and half between chicken pieces, and bake covered at 350° approximately 45 minutes. Uncover and spoon ½ cup sauce (from baking) into sour cream. Pour evenly over chicken sauce. (Optional: Sprinkle with 3 tablespoons bread crumbs blended with 1 tablespoon melted butter. Bake uncovered 15 to 20 minutes longer.)

Grand Tour Collection

Chicken Tetrazzini

My husband's Aunt Cynthia Fleming of Franklin, Tennessee, one of the best cooks in the world, told me when I first married that this dish would solve my entertaining problems and she was right. Tetrazzini like this may be made the day before and refrigerated or frozen and used weeks later. Served with a salad and French bread, this is a filling, delightful dinner.

2 cups chopped celery
1½ cups chopped onion
3 tablespoons butter or
  margarine
2 cups chicken broth
1 tablespoon Worcestershire
  sauce
Salt and pepper
1 (10½-ounce) can condensed
  cream of mushroom soup

½ cup milk
1 cup grated sharp cheese
½ pound spaghetti, cooked and
  drained
6 cups chopped, cooked chicken
½ cup sliced stuffed olive
1 cup chopped pecans

In a saucepan, cook celery and onion in butter until tender. Add chicken broth, Worcestershire sauce, salt, and pepper. Simmer about 15 minutes. Slowly stir in mushroom soup, milk, and cheese. Mix thoroughly. Remove from heat. Add cooked spaghetti. Let stand for 1 hour.

Preheat oven to 350°. Grease a 9 × 13-inch baking dish.

Add chicken and olives to spaghetti. Place in prepared dish. Sprinkle with chopped pecans. Bake 20 to 25 minutes or until hot and bubbly. Makes 12 servings.

Minnie Pearl Cooks

Chicken Rosemary

1 (2½-pound) chicken,
   disjointed
Salt
Pepper
1 medium onion, chopped
1 garlic clove, optional

½ stick butter
Flour
1 teaspoon rosemary
6 ounces sauterne or chablis
½ pint cream

Wash and dry chicken, sprinkle with salt and pepper. Lightly brown onion and crushed garlic in butter, using heavy skillet or Dutch oven. Add chicken, brown and dust both sides with flour and crushed rosemary. Add wine and cook covered in 300° oven for 45 minutes or until tender. Remove chicken to hot platter, add cream to sauce in skillet, heat and pour over chicken.

The Memphis Cookbook

Memphis displays its rich river heritage with the incredible Mud Island, just a monorail ride offshore from downtown, "in" the Mississippi River. The museum and theme park is a 50-acre tribute to the history and heritage of the "Father of Waters."

Skillet Fried Chicken

1 (2-pound) frying chicken, cut
  up or 2 pounds chicken parts
  (legs, thighs, and breasts)
¾ cup shortening or lard

1 cup flour mixed with 1½
  teaspoons salt and ½ teaspoon
  pepper

Roll chicken in flour mixture or place chicken and flour in bag and shake. Melt shortening in large heavy (preferably iron) skillet. Place chicken in (medium hot) fat and fry on one side for 10 minutes. Lower heat; cover and cook for 5 minutes. Turn chicken pieces and return heat to medium and fry on second side for 10 minutes. Lower heat, cover, and cook for 5 minutes. Cook uncovered a few minutes more for crispy crust. Remove chicken and drain on paper towels.

Drain fat from the skillet and save for CREAM GRAVY:

3 tablespoons fat
3 tablespoons flour
2 cups water or 1 cup milk and 1
  cup water

Salt and pepper

Return fat to skillet and add flour. Stir and scrape crusts from sides and bottom of skillet. Cook over low heat for 2–3 minutes. Add liquid, correct seasoning, and cook over medium heat for 3–4 minutes. Serve the gravy over hot biscuits, mashed potatoes, or rice. Serves 4–5.

The flavor of chicken is greatly improved if it is properly stored when purchased; that is, rinsed, drained, lightly salted, and stored in refrigerator overnight or soaked in cold salt water 1 hour before cooking.

The James K. Polk Cookbook

Kota Riganato
Chicken with Oregano

1 fryer chicken	1 clove garlic, minced
Salt and pepper to taste	4 tablespoons olive oil
1 lemon, juice of	½ stick butter
1 teaspoon oregano	

Season chicken with salt and pepper, lemon juice, oregano, garlic and oil. Dot with butter.

Bake at 350° until golden brown (approximately 1½ hours), basting frequently. Yield: 4 servings.

Note: Marinate overnight for richer flavor.

It's Greek to Me!

Country Style Chicken Kiev

¼ cup bread crumbs	⅔ cup butter, melted
2 tablespoons Parmesan cheese	2 whole chicken breasts
1 teaspoon basil	¼ cup white wine
1 teaspoon oregano	¼ cup green onion, chopped
½ teaspoon garlic salt	¼ cup fresh parsley, chopped
¼ teaspoon salt	

Combine bread crumbs, Parmesan cheese, basil, oregano, garlic salt and salt. Dip chicken pieces in butter then roll in crumb mixture. Set remaining butter aside. Place chicken skin side up in 2-quart shallow casserole. Bake at 375° for 50–60 minutes. To remaining butter add wine, green onions, and parsley. Pour over baked chicken and bake for 2–3 more minutes. Yield: 4 servings.

Upper Crust: A Slice of the South

Baked Chicken Breasts

12 chicken breasts (halves)
2 (10¾-ounce) cans cream of
chicken soup

½ pound shredded Swiss cheese
1 (10-ounce) bottle Durkee's
Famous Sauce

Skin chicken breasts and place in a 13 × 9 × 2-inch aluminum foil-lined baking pan. Combine remaining ingredients and pour over chicken. Cover with foil. Bake at 350° for 1½ hours. Serves 10 to 12.

Tennessee's 95 Magic Mixes: Second Helping

Chicken with Artichokes

6 chicken breasts, boned and
halved
1½ medium onions, sliced
1½ medium green peppers,
sliced
1½ sticks butter
½ cup olive oil
Juice of 1½ lemons

2½ cups uncooked rice
5 cups hot chicken broth
1 cup fresh mushrooms, sliced
1 tablespoon butter
12 canned artichoke hearts
Salt and pepper to taste
⅓ cup sliced, toasted almonds

Sauté chicken, onion and green pepper in butter and oil. Remove chicken, cover with lemon juice. Add rice and broth to the onion mixture; cook about 20 minutes. Remove from heat, add mushrooms which have been sautéed in 1 tablespoon butter, artichokes which have been drained and rinsed, salt and pepper. Place rice mixture and chicken in oblong baking dish, cover with foil, bake for 1 hour in 350° oven. Sprinkle almonds over casserole before serving. Serves 12.

Woman's Exchange Cookbook II

Chicken Ah-So

4–6 chicken breast halves, boned and skinned
2 tablespoons butter
1 (10¾-ounce) can Golden Mushroom Soup
½ cup water
1 beef bouillon cube
1 tablespoon soy sauce
1 teaspoon Worcestershire sauce
½ teaspoon curry powder
½ teaspoon poppy seeds
1 (8-ounce) can bamboo shoots, drained
½ cup sliced celery
1 small onion, sliced
1 (4-ounce) can sliced mushrooms, drained
1 small green pepper, cut in strips
3 tablespoons dry white wine
Cooked rice

Cut chicken into 1½-inch pieces and brown in butter until golden brown. Stir in next 7 ingredients and mix well. Cover and simmer for 15 minutes, stirring occasionally. Add next 6 ingredients. Cover and simmer 2–5 minutes longer. Serve over rice. Serves 4–6. Easy.

Well Seasoned

Rolled Chicken Breasts

½ cup Parmesan cheese, grated
¼ cup parsley, chopped
1 clove garlic, crushed
2 teaspoons salt
Red pepper to taste

6 chicken breast halves, boned
Melted butter or margarine
1 cup corn flakes, crushed
Chicken broth for basting

Mix first 5 ingredients. Dip chicken breasts in melted butter or margarine. Cover each piece completely with cheese mixture, then with corn flakes. Roll chicken breasts and secure with toothpicks. Bake at 350° for 1 hour, basting with chicken broth. Note: May use canned chicken broth, dissolved chicken bouillon cubes, or boil skin and bones from chicken breasts and make your own. Yield: 6 servings.

Dixie Delights

Chicken Supreme

4 supremes (boned chicken
   breasts from 2 fryers)
2 tablespoons butter or
   margarine
2 tablespoons oil
Salt and pepper to taste
¼ cup lemon juice

½ cup half-and-half or
   condensed milk
Parsley, chopped
½ pound fresh mushrooms,
   sliced
¼ cup green onion, chopped
2 tomatoes, peeled and chopped

Melt butter and oil in frying pan. Salt and pepper chicken fillets lightly. Sauté the supremes in fat 5–8 minutes on one side; turn the chicken and cook 5–6 minutes on the other side. They should be golden brown. Remove meat from pan; place on a platter.

Place onions, mushrooms, and tomatoes into fat remaining in the frying pan. Add lemon juice. Cook stirring continuously until fork tender (still crunchy). Slowly add ½ cup cream and parsley. Bring to simmer, but do not boil.

Place chicken on bed of cooked rice; pour the vegetable sauce over the chicken. Garnish with parsley, and sprinkle paprika on chicken. Serves 4.

Home Cooking in a Hurry

Kota Anginares Ke Manitaria
Chicken with Artichokes and Mushrooms

Salt to taste
Pepper to taste
Lawry's salt to taste
6 chicken breasts (or quarters)
1 stick butter
2 cans artichokes, drained,
　　reserve liquid

2 small jars mushrooms, drained
1 (3-ounce) can tomato paste
⅓ cup white wine
½ teaspoon Worcestershire sauce
¼ to ½ teaspoon oregano

Combine salt, pepper, and Lawry's salt and sprinkle over chicken; dot with butter and broil until brown. Remove from broiler, arrange artichokes and mushrooms around chicken.

Dilute tomato paste in juice of artichokes and ⅓ cup wine and Worcestershire sauce. Pour over broiled chicken. Sprinkle with oregano and bake at 350° for 45 minutes. Serve with rice or noodles. Yield: 6 servings.

It's Greek to Me!

Chicken-Beef Supreme

1 jar dried beef
4 deboned chicken beasts, split
¼ cup melted butter
½ cup Parmesan cheese

1 can cream of chicken soup
½ cup milk
½ cup grated Cheddar cheese

Preheat oven to 350°. Cover the bottom of a 9 × 13-inch casserole with all the beef. Rinse and drain the chicken beasts. Dip in melted butter and roll in Parmesan cheese. Place on top of dried beef. Heat chicken soup and milk until bubbly. Pour over chicken-beef combination. Sprinkle with grated cheese. Bake for 1 hour or until very tender.

Hint: Do not salt chicken due to beef being very salty.

Gazebo Gala

Quick and Easy Chicken Pot Pie

1 whole chicken, stewed and
    deboned, reserve broth
2 cups chicken broth
1 (10¾-ounce) can cream of
    chicken soup

Salt and pepper to taste
Celery salt (optional)
1½ cups biscuit mix
1½ cups milk
Butter or margarine

Place deboned chicken in bottom of greased 13 × 9 × 2-inch pan or
Pyrex dish. Mix broth and soup together and pour over chicken.
Season to taste. Mix biscuit mix and milk together. (Will form thin
mixture). Carefully pour over soup'and chicken mixture. Dot with
butter. Bake 1 hour at 350° or until brown. Yield: 6 to 8 servings.

Flaunting Our Finest

Granny Byrd's Chicken and Dumplings

When Lyman III was a student at the University of Mississippi, one of the men on the faculty wrote and thanked me for this recipe. He said for years his family had searched for a recipe to make dumplings like his grandmother served. He had tried my great-grandmother Byrd's recipe which we have handed down in our family. Mother was not too pleased when I made this dish on my television program and revealed another family secret.

3- or 4-pound hen	1 teaspoon salt
1 large onion	3 tablespoons cornstarch
2 cups all-purpose flour	⅓ cup cold water

Soak hen in cold salted water for several hours in refrigerator. Drain. Cook hen in fresh salted water after placing large whole peeled onion inside hen. Simmer, covered, about 3 or 4 hours, or until tender. Place hen in baking pan and remove broth from heat.

Put flour and salt in bowl. Skim about a cup or two of broth with chicken fat from top of liquid in pot and add to flour, mixing to make dough easily handled. Place on floured board. Put broth back over heat and bring to boil. Work flour-broth mixture into dough and roll thin. Cut into strips with knife and drop into rapidly boiling broth. Cook uncovered about 10 minutes or until dumplings are "set." Reduce heat, season with salt and black pepper, then make paste with cornstarch and cold water. Pour paste into broth, stirring to make gravy around dumplings. Cover pot and simmer slowly for 20–30 minutes, stirring occasionally to prevent sticking. Brown hen in oven, slice and serve on platter; pass dumplings in bowl.

Note: This makes a tender but chewy dumpling our family loves. One of my aunts says she adds a little yellow food coloring to make the dish look richer, but I think you would have to be careful and not overdo it. If you like light, fluffy dumplings, use self-rising flour, omit the salt, and follow the directions given above.

. . . and garnish with Memories

Sesame Chicken Nuggets

1 egg, slightly beaten
½ cup water
¾ teaspoon salt
¼ cup sesame seeds
½ cup flour

3 whole chicken breasts,
  skinned, boned and cut into 1-
  inch pieces
Vegetable oil for frying

Mix egg, water, salt, sesame seeds and flour to make a batter; stir in chicken pieces. Heat oil to medium. Carefully add chicken pieces, 1 layer at a time, frying until golden, about 3 to 5 minutes on each side. Drain on paper towels. Serve hot with toothpicks for dipping. Yield: Approximately 50 nuggets.

SAUCE PIQUANT:
½ cup apricot-pineapple
  preserves

2 tablespoons prepared mustard
2 tablespoons horseradish

Mix sauce ingredients in a small saucepan and cook for 3 minutes. Serve warm. Yield: ¾ cup.

Note: Nuggets may be frozen after frying. Thaw and reheat on a cookie sheet at 375° for about 10 minutes.

Out of this World

Chicken Kabobs

½ cup soy sauce
¼ teaspoon oil
½ cup water (or juice from
  pineapple and water)
1 clove garlic, minced
1 package Sweet 'n Low
¼ cup wine vinegar

¼ cup sherry
3 boned chicken breasts, cut in
  1-inch chunks
1 (8-ounce) can diet pack
  pineapple chunks
3 medium apples, cubed

Combine soy sauce, oil, water (or pineapple juice and water), garlic, Sweet 'n Low, wine vinegar and sherry. Add chicken, pineapple and apple. Marinate for 15 minutes. Alternate chicken, pineapple and apple on skewers. Broil approximately 15 minutes, basting occasionally with marinade. Serve with marinade for dipping. Serves 4. 281 calories per serving.

Southern Secrets

Chicken with Cashews

6 whole chicken breasts (3 pounds), skinned, boned and cut into ½-inch cubes
6 egg whites

6 tablespoons cornstarch
¾ teaspoon salt

SAUCE:
½ cup dry sherry
⅓ cup soy sauce
6 tablespoons sugar
6 tablespoons water

4 tablespoons cornstarch
3 tablespoons white vinegar
1 tablespoon sesame oil

Mix chicken pieces, egg whites, cornstarch and salt together by hand. In another bowl, combine sauce ingredients and mix well.

1 large green pepper, cut into ½-inch pieces
8 green onion bulbs, sliced thin
1 tablespoon ginger root, grated

2 cups corn oil
¾ cup dry roasted cashews
3 cloves garlic, peeled and minced

Prepare green pepper, green onion, and ginger root as indicated. Pour the corn oil into wok or heavy 10-inch skillet. Place over medium heat at 375°. Add chicken mixture, stirring constantly to separate pieces. Cook about 1 minute. Stir in green pepper and nuts. Remove from heat and drain mixture through colander into another pan. Discard all but about 2 tablespoons of oil. Set chicken mixture aside for the moment. Place wok with 2 tablespoons oil over heat again and add onion, garlic, and ginger. Cook about 1 minute. Then add chicken mixture and stir in sauce. Bring to boil, stirring constantly, and boil 1 minute. Serves 6.

NCJW Cookbook

Moon Mullican's Chicken and Pork Chops on Rice

My husband and I have many friends in country music. One of our favorites, who is no longer with us, was a delightful man named Moon Mullican.

Moon was always referred to as "the world's greatest hillbilly piano player," and he was. Moon and his wife, Eunice, used to come see us and either make or bring fabulous dishes that they learned to cook down around Port Arthur, Texas, and Louisiana. Moon had a wonderful recipe for Jambalaya which he used to cook all day long and while the food was cooking, we used to sing and play the piano and have a marvelous time. This recipe never had a name so we always called it Moon Mullican's Chicken and Pork Chops. I have never seen this dish cooked or served anywhere else. We always had just a salad and French bread with this dish.

I have not given amounts in this recipe because some people prefer more chicken than pork chops and vice versa. I prefer more chicken—naturally! This is not a hurry-up recipe. All afternoon produces the results.

Chopped onion	Chicken, cut up for frying
Chopped green pepper	Pork chops
Chopped celery	Salt and pepper
Cooking oil	Flour
Small clove garlic, minced	Hot, cooked rice

In Dutch oven or large heavy skillet with lid, sauté equal amount of each chopped vegetable in small amount of oil. Add garlic to taste. Season chicken and pork chops with salt and pepper. Brown slowly in oil with vegetables. Cover and cook very slowly on top of range or in 300° oven all afternoon (at least 3 hours). Add water sparingly if needed. (Chicken bouillon may be used instead of water.) At serving time, remove meat from Dutch oven. Remove bones. It will be so tender bones can be very easily removed.

SAUCE:
Add enough flour to cooked liquid to thicken. Season as desired. Heat and stir until smooth. Combine with meat. Serve over hot, cooked rice.

Minnie Pearl Cooks

Southern Chicken Stew

4 pounds stewing chicken	2 large onions
⅓ cup flour	2¼ teaspoons salt
1 teaspoon salt	¼ teaspoon pepper
⅓ cup fat	1 pound tender okra
3 cups water	1 tablespoon flour
1½ pounds tomatoes, 4 medium	¼ cup water

Choose chicken for stewing. Singe, clean and wash. Dredge with flour and the 1 teaspoon salt mixed. Brown slowly in hot fat in a large heavy skillet or Dutch oven. Add 3 cups water, cover, reduce heat. Simmer gently for 1 hour. Add peeled, sliced tomatoes, sliced peeled onions and remaining salt and pepper. Continue to simmer until chicken is nearly tender enough to serve. Twenty minutes before chicken is to be served, add trimmed, sliced okra pods on top of stew and cook uncovered for remaining time. Add flour to the ¼ cup cold water and blend until smooth; stir gently into stew, stirring constantly and cook until stew thickens slightly. Serve at once. 6 servings.

Tennessee Treasure

Turkey and Wild Rice Casserole

2 cups long grain wild rice
1 onion, chopped
2 tablespoons butter or
    margarine
½ cup flour
9 ounces mushrooms, sliced
3 cups half and half*

6 cups turkey, diced**
1 cup slivered almonds, toasted
½ cup pimento, diced
4 tablespoons parsley
Salt and pepper
Breadcrumbs

Prepare rice according to package directions. Sauté onions in butter, remove from heat and stir in flour. Drain mushrooms, save liquid. Combine that liquid with cream and enough liquids to make 4 cups. Stir slowly into flour mixture. Cook and stir until thick. Add rice, mushrooms, turkey (chicken), toasted almonds, pimento, parsley, salt and pepper. Put in a 9 × 12 × 2-casserole, top with buttered breadcrumbs and bake 40 minutes at 350°. This may be prepared the day before, and frozen.

*Use one pint half-and-half plus chicken broth to make 3 cups.
**You can do this with chicken as well.

Joyce's Favorite Recipes

Allen's Honey Duck

1 wild duck
2 teaspoons plus ⅛ teaspoon salt
½ teaspoon pepper
1 teaspoon ground ginger
1 teaspoon ground basil
1–2 oranges
¾ cup honey

¼ cup butter
3 tablespoons orange juice
2 tablespoons lemon juice
1 tablespoon grated orange peel
⅛ teaspoon dry mustard
½ teaspoon cornstarch

Combine salt, pepper, ginger, and basil. Rub some of this mixture inside duck. (Reserve remaining mixture.) Slice unpeeled oranges ½-inch thick, stuff as many as possible inside duck. Combine and heat remaining ingredients, pour 2 or 3 tablespoons inside duck. Truss duck, rub rest of dry seasonings over outside. Seal duck in aluminum foil, bake for 1¼ hours at 325°. Unwrap, baste with any remaining honey mixture. Bake 20 to 25 minutes more until browned.

Woman's Exchange Cookbook II

Delicious Ducks

2 good-sized ducks (i.e. mallards)
Salt and pepper
½ cup melted butter
¼ cup soy sauce
1 orange, whole

2 tablespoons orange marmalade
1 cup water
1 (6-ounce) can frozen orange juice concentrate, thawed

Wash and dry ducks. Salt and pepper liberally inside and out. Brush with melted butter and soy sauce. Put ½ orange and 1 tablespoon marmalade in each body cavity. Place both ducks in pressure cooker or crock pot. Pour remaining butter and soy sauce over ducks. Pour 1 cup water in bottom. Pour orange juice concentrate (undiluted) over ducks. Cook 45 minutes in pressure cooker; 45 minutes on high for crock pot, then 3 to 4 hours on medium heat. After cooking is complete, remove duck meat from bones, saving juice in pan. Thicken juice with small amount of flour and water paste. Mix with duck meat. Serve over rice. Garnish with orange slices and parsley. Freezes well. Serves 4.

Southern Secrets

Roast Goose

1 goose	½ teaspoon cinnamon
1 clove garlic	2 anise seeds
2 teaspoons olive oil	¾ cup soy sauce
½ cup chopped onion	1 tablespoon sugar
¼ cup chopped celery	2 cups hot water

Mix all ingredients together and fill cavity of goose. Sew or skewer together so juice cannot run out. Place in roaster and bake at 350° until tender, basting frequently with the following mixture:

2 cups boiling water	¼ cup vinegar
½ cup honey	1 tablespoon soy sauce

Goose should roast tender in about 3½ hours. Drain liquid from goose and chicken for gravy with cornstarch.

World's Fair Cookbook

Rock Cornish Game Hens

Season each hen with salt, pepper and butter inside and out. Place 1 tablespoon butter on each breast; wrap tightly in foil, cook for 1 hour in 350° oven. Open foil, return to oven, baste frequently with Cumberland Sauce until nicely glazed and brown—about 15 minutes.

CUMBERLAND SAUCE:

For each hen:

1 tablespoon butter	1 tablespoon cornstarch
¼ cup currant jelly	½ cup port wine
1 tablespoon lemon juice	

Combine first three ingredients, simmer, then thicken with cornstarch, using a little hot jelly sauce to blend cornstarch. Add port and heat.

Woman's Exchange Cookbook II

Meats

Tennessee's beautiful caves, mountains, rivers and valleys offer a virtual paradise of unspoiled wilderness for hikers and campers.

Beef Balls with Pineapple and Peppers

BEEF BALLS:

1 pound ground beef
1 tablespoon cornstarch
2 tablespoons onion, chopped
1 teaspoon salt

Few grains ginger and freshly
  ground pepper
1 egg

Mix together and form into small balls. Brown in about 1 table-spoon oil. Drain and put aside.

SAUCE:

1 tablespoon oil
1 cup pineapple juice
3 tablespoons cornstarch
1 tablespoon soy sauce
3 tablespoons vinegar

6 tablespoons water
½ cup sugar
2 green peppers, cut in thin
  slices
1 can diced pineapple cubes

To oil, add the pineapple juice and cook over low heat for a few minutes. Mix together the cornstarch, soy sauce, vinegar, water, and sugar. Add to juice and cook until it thickens, stirring constantly. This dish may be made in advance up to this point. Add the meat balls, the diced pineapple, and green peppers. Heat thoroughly. Serve hot. It is very suitable for a chafing dish.
    Serves 6 to 8.

NCJW Cookbook

Meat Loaf

1 pound lean ground beef
1 egg, beaten
1 teaspoon salt
¼ cup catsup

¼ pound hot sausage
½ cup bread or cracker crumbs
¼ teaspoon black pepper
¼ cup milk

Combine all ingredients and shape into a loaf. Place loaf in lightly greased pan and bake approximately 1 hour at 350°. When loaf is done, pour small can of tomato sauce, lightly salted and with one teaspoon lemon juice, over it. Return to oven until sauce is heated, approximately 10 minutes.

Elvis Fans Cookbook

Smoky Barbecued Meatloaf

MEATLOAF:

1 pound ground lean beef
1 egg
1 cup low-sodium bread crumbs

1 medium onion, chopped
Pepper to taste

SAUCE:

1 (4-ounce) can tomato puree, unsalted
3 tablespoons firmly packed brown sugar
1 tablespoon low-sodium prepared mustard

½ cup vinegar
1 teaspoon liquid smoke
1 teaspoon Mrs. Dash (14 herb and spice blend)

Mix ingredients for meatloaf with half the sauce mixture. Shape into two loaves and place in 12-inch iron skillet. Pour remaining sauce over meatloaf and bake at 325° for 1 hour. Yield: 6 servings. Serving: 3 ounces-60 milligrams sodium, 260 calories.

Tip: Cooking in iron utensils increases iron content of food. Iron is a nutrient often deficient in our diet.

Change of Seasons

Mom's Hamburgers

1 pound ground beef
1 beaten egg
½ teaspoon salt (or to taste)
Dash pepper
¾ cup cornflakes

2 tablespoons minced onion
1½ tablespoon Worcestershire sauce
¼ cup bottled chili sauce
¼ cup barbecue sauce (Kraft)

Combine ingredients. Mix thoroughly. Form into 6 or 7 patties. Broil 3 to 5 inches from heat. Broil about 8 to 10 minutes, turn, broil 5 to 7 minutes. Serve on Roman Meal buns (or white buns). The young people especially like my hamburgers. They always call them Mom's Hamburgers.

Family Favorites by the Miller's Daughters

Trashburger Cooker

1 galvanized bucket
1 church key
1 double grill (the kind with
  long handles that looks like 2
  square tennis rackets hinged
  together)

8 or 9 double pages of
  newspaper wadded up

With the church key, punch 4 or 5 holes in the bottom of the bucket. Discard church key and reserve the bucket. Sandwich 4 or 5 hamburger patties in the grill. Put 6 of the paper wads into the bucket and light them. Hold ,the burgers over the fire. Soon you have a grease fire going that would be the envy of the Dobbs House grill! The bigger the better! If it dies down before 5 minutes on each side, add more paper wads, one at a time.

This method offends most purists of the "glowing coals" school, but it is a fast, cheap method, and most people can't tell the difference!

A Man's Taste

108

Ground Beef, Corn and Cheese Bake

This recipe was a First Place Winner in the Dairy Recipe Contest for Monroe County.

3 tablespoons butter
3½ pounds ground beef
3¾ cups fresh whole kernel corn, or 3 (10-ounce) packages frozen corn, partly thawed
3 (15-ounce) cans tomato sauce
1 teaspoon garlic salt
¾ teaspoon black pepper
2 tablespoons dried oregano leaves

1 tablespoon sugar
16 ounces noodles (medium), cooked
3½ cups cottage cheese
3 (8-ounce) packages cream cheese, softened
1½ cups sour cream
4½ cups Cheddar cheese, grated

Line three 8 × 8 × 2-inch baking dishes with freezer wrap. (Do not line fourth baking dish, which is to be used for food to be served without freezing.) Melt butter in large skillet; add ground beef and cook over medium heat until browned, stirring with a fork to separate. Remove meat with slotted spoon to drain. Pour off pan drippings and put meat back into skillet; stir in corn, tomato sauce, garlic salt, black pepper, oregano and sugar; cook over moderate heat for 5 minutes. Remove skillet from heat. Cook noodles as directed on package; drain. Mix cottage cheese, cream cheese and sour cream in a large mixing bowl; then mix with cooked noodles. Layer half the noodle-cheese mixture in the bottom of the 4 casserole dishes; cover with half the meat sauce and sprinkle ⅓ cup grated cheese on each casserole. Add remaining noodle-cheese mixture, and then meat sauce. Sprinkle each with remaining grated cheese.

To bake without freezing: heat oven to 350°. Bake casserole uncovered 40 to 45 minutes, until bubbly and lightly browned.

To freeze: fold and seal freezer wrap on remaining casseroles. Label and freeze.

To bake after freezing: heat oven to 350°. Remove freezer wrap from frozen casserole. Place, still frozen, in original baking dish. Bake uncovered 1 hour and 15 minutes, or until heated through and lightly brown.

Note: The size of the baking dish can be adjusted to the number of servings needed each time.

The Original Tennessee Homecoming Cookbook

Ground Beef Stroganoff

¼ cup (½ stick) butter or
  margarine
½ cup finely chopped onion or 2
  teaspoons instant minced
  onion
1 pound ground beef
2 tablespoons flour
1 (8-ounce) can mushroom
  stems and pieces, drained

1 teaspoon salt
1 (10½-ounce) can condensed
  cream of chicken soup,
  undiluted
1 cup buttermilk
Chopped parsley for garnish

In a large skillet, melt butter. Add onion and cook until transparent. Add meat and heat until it loses red color. Stir in flour, drained mushrooms, and salt. Cook 5 minutes. Add soup; simmer an additional 10 minutes. Stir in buttermilk and heat to desired serving temperature. Do not boil. Serve over noodles or rice. Garnish with parsley. Serves 6–8.

To freeze, remove from heat after adding buttermilk. Cool. Package and freeze. When ready to use, defrost in refrigerator for 5 hours or more. Heat only until bubbly.

The Nashville Cookbook

No Peep Stew

2 pounds lean beef
2 cups Irish potatoes
2 cups celery
2 cups chopped onions
2 cups chopped carrots
Lowery's seasoning salt

3 cans Snap-E-Tom tomato
  cocktail
3 tablespoons tapioca
Salt
Pepper

Cube and mix together meat and vegetables. Season to taste with salt, pepper and Lowery's and any other desired seasoning. Place in a Dutch oven. Dissolve tapioca in the tomato juice and pour over mixture. Bake for 5 hours at 250°. Do Not Peep! Serves 6–8.

Maury County Cookbook

Cabbage Rolls

1 large head of cabbage   2 cups beef broth

With a sharp knife remove the core and drop the cabbage, core side down, into a kettle of boiling, salted water to cover and blanch it for 5 to 6 minutes, or until the leaves are softened. Drain and carefully separate the leaves.

FILLING:

¼ cup margarine   1 beaten egg
1 tablespoon paprika   2 tablespoons minced fresh
½ cup finely chopped onion   parsley
1 pound ground beef   Salt and pepper to taste
2 cups cooked rice

Melt margarine in skillet; add paprika and chopped onion; cook for 5 minutes. Remove from heat. Add remaining ingredients and mix all together.

Put 2 heaping tablespoons of the filling on each leaf and roll the leaves up tightly, tucking the ends under. Arrange rolls seam side down in greased 3-quart casserole or medium size roaster. Pour 2 cups beef broth* over rolls and bake covered at 350° for 1 hour. Thicken gravy and serve over the rolls. If desired, sour cream may be added to the gravy.

*BEEF BROTH SUBSTITUTE:

1 large can drained sauerkraut   1 tablespoon brown sugar
2 (8-ounce) cans tomato sauce

Layer half the sauerkraut in bottom of casserole dish and the other half on top of rolls. Pour tomato sauce over rolls and sprinkle brown sugar over. Bake same as above.

Das Germantown Kochbuch

Chinese Delight T-Bone Steak

2 tablespoons crushed fresh
  ginger root
4 cloves garlic, crushed
2 tablespoons dry sherry
1 tablespoon sugar
2 tablespoons dark soy sauce
1 tablespoon cornstarch

2 pounds T-bone steak
½ cup oil
½ cup light soy sauce
1 tablespoon sesame seed oil
2 scallions, cut in 2-inch pieces
  and shredded

Mix ginger root, garlic, dry sherry, sugar and dark soy sauce with cornstarch. Coat both sides of steak with mixture and marinate overnight or 2 hours minimum. Heat ½ cup oil in frying pan on very high heat. Brown both sides of steak. Broil steak in oven on a rack in a baking pan. Turn a few times. Cook steak to the way desired. For crispness, set oven on 500° for the last 5 minutes with oven door half open. Add light soy sauce and sesame seed oil to frying pan with remaining oil. Bring to a boil. Cut steak and pour sauce on the steak. Sprinkle shredded scallions over it. Serve hot with rice. Serves 4 to 6.

Elvis Fans Cookbook II

Braised Sirloin Tips on Rice

2 tablespoons shortening
1½ pounds stew beef
1 can condensed beef consomme
⅓ cup water
2 tablespoons soy sauce

¼ teaspoon onion salt
Dash garlic salt
2 tablespoons cornstarch
¼ cup water

Melt shortening. Brown meat. Stir in consomme, ⅓ cup water, soy sauce, and salts. Heat to boiling. Reduce heat; cover and simmer 1 hour or until meat is tender. Blend cornstarch and ¼ cup water. Stir gradually into meat mixture. Cook, stirring constantly until mixture boils. Boil and stir 1 minute. Serve over rice.

Koinonia Cooking

Boeuf Bourguignon
Beef Bourbon

5 medium-sized onions, chopped
2 tablespoons bacon drippings
2 pounds lean beef, cubed
1½ tablespoons flour
½ teaspoon thyme
Salt to taste

Pepper to taste
½ teaspoon marjoram
½ cup beef bouillon
1 cup dry red wine
½ pound fresh mushrooms
4 ounces bourbon whiskey

Fry onions in bacon drippings. Remove to separate dish. Sauté beef in bacon drippings. Sprinkle with flour, thyme, salt, pepper, and marjoram. Add ½ cup bouillon and 1 cup wine. Simmer 3½ hours very slowly. Add half bouillon and wine if more liquid is needed as it cooks. Add browned onions and mushrooms. Cook 30 minutes longer. Sauce should be thick and dark brown. Add 4 ounces bourbon and serve immediately.

One cup sour cream may be added if you would like to change recipe to stroganoff.

World's Fair Cookbook

Parmesan Round Steak

1½ pounds round steak cut ¾
   inches thick
1 egg, beaten
⅓ cup milk
½ cup fine dry bread crumbs
Salt
⅛ teaspoon pepper

1 tablespoon Accent seasoning
3 tablespoons bacon drippings
½ cup water
¼ teaspoon leaf oregano
¼ cup grated Parmesan cheese
¼ teaspoon paprika
6 small onions

Cut steak into 6 serving pieces. Pound to ½-inch thickness. Combine egg and milk. Mix bread crumbs, 1 teaspoon salt, pepper and Accent. Dip steaks in egg mixture, dredge with seasoned crumbs. Brown meat in drippings, add water. Sprinkle oregano on steaks. Place 2 teaspoons Parmesan cheese on each steak. Combine ¼ teaspoon salt and paprika. Sprinkle onions with salt mixture. Add to meat, cover tightly. Bake for 1½ to 2 hours in a 325° oven.

Recipes from Miss Daisy's

Beef Roulades
Father Bernard's

3 pounds round steak, about ¼-inch thick
6 strips bacon or salt pork
¼ cup butter or margarine
1 cup sliced onions

1 cup beef broth
2 cups dry red wine
1 bay leaf
1 tablespoon cornstarch
2 tablespoons water

FILLING:
½ pound sausage
5 tablespoons crumbled cornbread

Mix filling ingredients together. Pound steak thin enough to stuff and roll easily; cut into 4 × 5-inch pieces. Place about 1 rounded tablespoon of filling on each beef slice; roll up from short end. Wrap each with strip of bacon or salt pork; fasten with a toothpick.

In Dutch oven, brown roulades in butter or margarine. Remove roulades and set aside. Add onions, sauté until transparent. Place roulades on top of onions, pour over beef broth and red wine. Add bay leaf. Bring to a boil and simmer covered 1½ to 2 hours, or until meat is fork tender. Remove bay leaf. Thicken gravy with cornstarch dissolved in water.

SAUTÉED VEGETABLES:
3 cups onions, thinly sliced
1 (2½-ounce) jar sliced mushrooms

½ cup butter or margarine

Sauté vegetables in butter till transparent.

To serve: Remove toothpicks from roulades. Arrange in center of a large, heated platter; surround with onions and mushrooms. Spoon some of sauce over all. Sprinkle vegetables with chopped parsley. Pass rest of gravy. Makes about 6 servings.

Das Germantown Kochbuch

Beef Carbonnade

¼ pound bacon
3 pounds round steak, cubed
2 large onions, chopped
2 tablespoons butter
2 tablespoons flour
1 (12-ounce) can warm beer
1 teaspoon salt

1 teaspoon sugar
1 clove garlic, minced
½ teaspoon pepper
½ teaspoon thyme
½ teaspoon rosemary
½ teaspoon marjoram

Cook bacon until crisp; remove from skillet and save. Brown round steak and onions in bacon drippings; place meat and onions in casserole. Mix butter, flour and beer in another skillet, add remaining ingredients. Pour over meat and cook, covered, in 325° oven for 2½ hours. Before serving you may want to add some more warm beer to thin liquid. Sprinkle crumbled bacon over meat. Serves 6 to 8.

Cantaloupe or honeydew melon slices make a great accompaniment to this recipe.

Woman's Exchange Cookbook II

Chuck Wagon Pepper Steak

1 chuck roast (4–5 pounds)
2 teaspoons unseasoned meat
   tenderizer
2 tablespoons instant minced
   onion
2 teaspoons thyme

1 teaspoon marjoram
1 bay leaf, crushed
1 cup wine vinegar
½ cup olive or salad oil
3 tablespoons lemon juice
¼ cup peppercorns

Sprinkle meat evenly on both sides with tenderizer. Pierce deeply all over with fork. Place in a shallow pan. Mix remaining ingredients and pour over and around meat. Refrigerate 5–6 hours ('the longer the better), turning occasionally. Cook over hot coals 45 minutes to 1 hour, basting with marinade. Serves 6–8.

The James K. Polk Cookbook

Barbecued Roast

1 (3–4-pound) beef roast
2 teaspoons salt
¼ teaspoon pepper
3 tablespoons fat
½ cup water
1 (8-ounce) can tomato sauce
3 medium onions
2 cloves of garlic

2 tablespoons brown sugar
½ teaspoon mustard
¼ cup lemon juice
¼ cup catsup
¼ cup vinegar
1 tablespoon Worcestershire
   sauce

Rub meat with salt, and pepper, brown in fat, add water, tomato sauce and thinly sliced onions and minced garlic. Cover and cook over low heat on top of stove for 1½ hours. Combine remaining ingredients and pour over the meat. Cover and continue cooking about 1 hour or until tender.

Note: Let your roast stand at room temperature about 1 hour before cooking.

Parties & Pleasures

Fool Proof Rare Beef Roast

**1 boneless rolled rump roast, no
less than 3¾ pounds or 1
boneless rolled English cut
roast, no less than 3¾ pounds
or 2, 3, or 4-rib roast or
sirloin tip roast**

Proceed with following instructions the night before planning to
serve roast. Preheat oven to 375°. Rub roast with salt and pepper;
place on rack in roasting pan. Bake exactly 1 hour. Turn oven off.
Do not open oven door during cooking nor during night. Roast
may be removed from oven during the day, if oven is needed.

To make pan juice gravy, remove cooked roast from pan, add 1
cup water for smaller roasts, 2 cups for larger roasts. Stir with a
spoon over low heat to loosen juices cooked to pan. Correct seasoning to taste. Pour into sauce pan to reheat at time of serving.

Before serving, place roast in cold oven. Turn oven to 300°. Heat
for 22 minutes for 2-rib roast or 4-pound rolled roast; 25 to 30
minutes for 3-rib roast or 6-pound rolled roast; 35 minutes for 4-
rib roast or 8-pound rolled roast. Serve immediately. Allow ½
pound meat per person.

Woman's Exchange Cookbook II

---

*More than 900 miles of hiking trails meander through the 500,000 acres of wilderness in
the Great Smoky Mountain National Park. The Cherokee Indians called this land
Shaconage—"Place of the Blue Smoke."*

Ice Cream Salt Roast

Beef roast   Pepper
Salt   Praise Allah (optional)

Wash and drain roast. Sprinkle both sides lightly with salt, pepper and Praise Allah seasoning. Cover bottom of small roaster with ice cream salt. Place roast in roasting pan on top of salt. Cover completely with ice cream salt. Sprinkle well with water. Place in 475° oven. Bake 15 minutes per pound. Remove from oven. Crack salt with hammer and enjoy the nice juicy and delicious roast.*

    *The roast does not absorb the ice cream salt—only locks in the delicious juice and flavor.

Our Favorite Recipes

Boiled Beef Dinner and Pot Liquor with Cornmeal Dumplings

5–6 pound pot roast or brisket	8 onions, cut
8 cups water	8 white turnips, cut
8 carrots, cut	1 cabbage head, cut in 8 pieces
8 parsnips, cut	Salt and pepper to taste

Put roast or brisket in pot with 8 cups water. Cover tightly and simmer 4 hours. Remove meat and simmer all the vegetables except cabbage in seasoned broth until tender. Place vegetables in roaster with meat and cover to keep warm. Cook cabbage. Do not over-cook. Place in roaster.

Now make dumplings and cook in broth.

CORNMEAL DUMPLINGS:

2 eggs, beaten	1 cup flour
½ cup milk	½ teaspoon salt
2 tablespoons melted butter	2 teaspoons baking powder
1 cup white cornmeal	

Beat eggs; add milk, butter and rest of the ingredients. Shape into 16 balls. Roll in more cornmeal. Drop all at once in broth or pot liquor. Simmer 15 minutes.

Now place meat, vegetables and dumplings on a big platter. Thicken pot liquor. Pour over top and serve with salt and black pepper.

Kountry Kooking

Brisket of Beef a la Bercy

2 teaspoons salt
3 tablespoons brown sugar
1 (12-ounce) bottle chili sauce
1½ cups vinegar
2 teaspoons season salt

6–8 tablespoons liquid smoke
1 large brisket
1 cup chopped celery and leaves
2 sliced onions

Mix salt, brown sugar, chili sauce, vinegar, season salt, and liquid smoke together. Pour over beef. Cover with celery and onions. Roast at 325° until tender. Cover if meat gets too brown.

NCJW Cookbook

Souvlakia II
Shish-Ka-Bob

2 pounds lamb or beef
2 cloves garlic, minced
½ cup salad oil
1 cup Burgundy wine
1 lemon, juice of
Salt and pepper to taste
2 teaspoons oregano

3 tomatoes (optional)
2 onions (optional)
4 strips bacon (optional)
2 bell peppers (optional)
1 can whole mushroom buttons
  or use fresh (optional)

Cut meat into 1½-inch cubes. Place meat in large plastic or stainless steel bowl and add garlic, oil, wine, lemon juice, salt, pepper and oregano, and mix well. Cover and refrigerate overnight to marinate.

Quarter tomatoes and onion; cube bacon and peppers. Skewer marinated meat alternating it with whichever optional ingredients are preferred. Charcoal over hot coals or broil in oven to desired doneness. Yield: 8 servings.

It's Greek to Me!

Wiener Schnitzel

6 veal chops or steaks	3 tablespoons bacon drippings
Salt and pepper	Juice of 1 lemon
2 eggs, slightly beaten	1 tablespoon flour
Flour	1 cup thick sour cream

Sprinkle veal with salt and pepper. Dip into eggs; then into flour. Brown on both sides in bacon drippings. Cover and cook slowly until meat is tender, about 1 hour. Sprinkle with lemon juice and arrange on a hot platter. Blend flour with fat in pan; add sour cream and cook for 3 minutes; stir constantly. Season with salt and pepper; pour over chops.

Das Germantown Kochbuch

Veal Modena

6 veal cutlets	2 tablespoons bacon fat
Salt and pepper	1 small onion, chopped
1 egg	3 tablespoons Marsala wine
Bread crumbs	1 tablespoon tomato paste
6 tablespoons butter	½ cup chicken stock

Beat cutlets thin and nick edges with a knife so they won't curl up. Salt and pepper them, dip into beaten egg and then into bread crumbs. Heat the butter and bacon fat together and sauté onion. Add cutlets and brown them. Add wine and cook until evaporated. Add tomato paste to stock and cook another 10 minutes or until tender.

Grand Tour Collection

Veal Scallopini with Tomatoes

1½ pounds veal, sliced, cut in 1-inch pieces and pounded
¾ cup all-purpose flour
2 tablespoons butter
1 tablespoon olive oil
½ pound mushrooms, thinly sliced
½–1 clove garlic, minced
2 tablespoons chopped fresh parsley
1–2 tablespoons chopped fresh basil
½ cup peeled, seeded, diced, fresh tomatoes
½ cup Marsala wine
2 tablespoons grated in Parmesan cheese

Preheat oven to 325°. Dredge veal squares in flour. Brown veal in butter and oil in large frying pan. Add mushrooms and cook 5 minutes. Add garlic, parsley and basil. Cook 1 minute. Add tomatoes and cook 5 minutes. Stir in Marsala. Remove to baking platter. Sprinkle Parmesan on top. Bake for 45 minutes. Yield: 4 servings.

Dinner on the Diner

Sausage Stroganoff

1 clove garlic
2 pounds country sausage
3 tablespoons flour
2 cups milk
2 large onions, sliced then
  chopped

1 large can mushrooms
⅛ pound butter
2 teaspoons soy sauce
2 tablespoons Worcestershire
Salt, pepper, paprika to taste
1 pint sour cream

Rub large skillet with garlic and heat. Brown sausage well. Pour off grease as it accumulates. Dredge sausage with flour. Add milk and simmer until slightly thickened. Set aside.

Sauté onions and mushrooms in butter. To the sausage-cream sauce mixture add soy sauce, Worcestershire, onions, mushrooms and seasonings. When mixture bubbles, add sour cream. Keep hot in chafing dish. Heap upon biscuits or pastry shells or use as a dip with Melba toast. Wonderful served in chafing dish for cocktail parties, large or small!

For 50 people or over, double recipe. When doubling, add only 3 onions. May be made in advance and frozen, eliminating sour cream. On day of party, thaw and heat in electric skillet, adding sour cream as called for in recipe. Remains from party can be served over rice for dinner. Served with rice, this will serve 6.

Party Potpourri

Saucy Sausage

2 pounds sausage (hot or mild)
1 cup sour cream
1 (9-ounce) bottle chutney,
  chopped

½ cup dry sherry

Shape sausage into small balls and cook. (May be frozen at this point if desired.)

Mix sour cream, chutney and sherry. Put into chafing dish. Add sausage balls. Serve with toothpicks. Yield: 20 servings.

This is excellent over rice as a main dish. Sausage links may be substituted for bulk sausage.

Dinner on the Diner

Boxcar Barbecue

6 pound Boston butt pork roast
1 (28-ounce) can whole peeled
  tomatoes, mashed
½ cup vinegar
1 (5-ounce) bottle soy sauce

1 (5-ounce) bottle
  Worcestershire sauce
½ cup brown sugar
4 medium onions, chopped

Place roast in roasting pan. Mix all other ingredients and pour over roast. Bake at 300° for 4 to 5 hours. Remove all bones and shred meat. Freezes well. Yield: 8–10 servings.

Dinner on the Diner

Stuffed Roast Loin of Pork
Super duper

1 whole or half pork loin
Apple rings
Cornbread top-of-stove stuffing
  mix

Honey and lemon juice

Have butcher loosen backbone from ribs and cut loin into 6 to 8 chops, but not through to the bone. Pare and core apples, one fewer than number of chops; slice in ½-inch thick rings. Prepare stuffing mix according to directions for moist mixture. Place an apple ring and a spoonful of stuffing between chops, beginning and ending with a chop. Tie together with a clean white string or hold together with skewers. Place in roasting pan. Roast at 325° about 2 hours, basting occasionally with honey mixed with a little lemon juice. Remove string or skewers and serve at once with cranberry relish.

Sam Houston Schoolhouse Cookbook

Sweet Ham and Pork Loaf

2 pounds ground cured ham	1 cup milk
1½ pounds ground pork steak	1 cup cracker or bread crumbs
2 beaten eggs	Salt and pepper

To the ground meat add the beaten eggs, milk, crumbs and mix thoroughly. Salt and pepper to taste. Make into a loaf. Place in 350° oven and when slightly browned baste frequently with the following syrup:

1½ cups brown sugar	½ cup vinegar
1 tablespoon mustard	½ cup water

Combine the ingredients and cook 5 minutes. Use for basting the meat loaf. Bake 2 hours. Serve hot or cold.

Smoky Mountain Magic

Sweet 'n Sour Chops

6 butterfly (boneless) pork chops	¼ cup ketchup
1 (10½-ounce) can beef consommé	2 tablespoons wine vinegar
	1 tablespoon brown sugar
½ cup drained pineapple chunks	1 teaspoon soy sauce
¼ cup chopped green pepper	½ teaspoon dry mustard

Brown chops in fry pan; pour off excess fat. Arrange chops in 13 × 9 × 2-inch casserole. Combine consommé, pineapple, chopped pepper, ketchup, wine vinegar, brown sugar, soy sauce and dry mustard. Pour over chops and bake uncovered in 400° oven for 45 minutes. Serves 6.

Southern Secrets

Mel's Country Summer Day Dinner

6 center cut pork chops
Turnip greens
6 medium turnips
1 teaspoon sugar
2 cups water
10 pieces white bacon

Serve with:
Potato salad
Beets
Cornbread
Green onions
Blackberry cobbler

First, stem greens and pick out old or tough leaves. Wash greens thoroughly 3 times. Remove all the dirt and bugs and all the other little critters. Mama says, "The dirt and grit causes kidney stones and gall stones," so Mama says to wash the greens 3 times and if you didn't she'd get you! Now, after you've picked and stemmed and washed the greens real good, put them in a large cooking pot. Peel and slice the turnips into ¼" chips. Layer them along with the 6 porkchops in with the greens. Mama says, "The secret to good greens is 1 teaspoon of sugar and no salt at all." Mama lets you salt your own. Put about 2 cups of water into the pot. The water keeps the greens from burning and the stem helps wilt the greens down to start cooking in their own juices. Next, slice off about 10 pieces of white bacon and place the pieces in a skillet and cook until all the fat has rendered out of the bacon. Pour hot bacon grease over the greens. Put the bacon on a plate to be served at meal time also. Cover pot with a lid and cook greens on high until water starts to boil, then turn down the heat to low. Mama says, "It takes about 45 minutes to 1 hour to make good greens." It depends on how tender you want them. Don't you take that lid off until they're done, 'les' you want to get your hand slapped!

Serve with: Iced tea, bread and butter pickles, pickled hot pepper sauce (to pour over greens) and applesauce. "Mama says, 'Serve applesauce to help digest the pork chops, else you'll get trichinosis,' whatever that is!"

Mel Tillis, Elvis Fans Cookbook II

How to Cook a Country Ham

1 (20–22 pound) country ham	2 bay leaves
1 cup pickle juice, *or* ½ cup apple	Mustard
vinegar	Brown sugar
1 red pepper pod, seeds removed	Sifted bread crumbs
1 lemon, quartered	½ cup sherry
1 onion, halved	Whole cloves

Scrub ham in cold water with stiff brush; soak overnight in cold water, making certain that the ham is completely covered. Remove ham and place it in a covered lard stand or large ham boiler, skin side down. Barely cover with fresh water to which pickle juice, pepper pod, lemon, onion, and bay leaves have been added. Let come to a boil and lower heat to medium. Ham is done when large flat bone can be removed with your fingers—this takes less than 15 minutes per pound. When done, remove lid and cool ham in liquid in which it is cooked. When ham is cool, skin off the rind and lightly pierce the fat side. Rub ham with mustard and pat on brown sugar. Sprinkle with bread crumbs and pour sherry over entire top of ham. Stick with whole cloves and brown lightly in a 400° oven. Let cool for at least 12 hours before slicing. Preparation time: 1½ days.

Nashville Seasons

Ham Tetrazzini

1 (8-ounce) can mushrooms	1 chicken bouillon cube
(stems, pieces or sliced)	1 (7-ounce) package thin
1 small onion, diced	spaghetti, broken into 2-inch
¼ cup melted margarine	pieces and cooked
¼ cup flour	2 cups cooked ham, diced
1 teaspoon dry mustard	¼ cup shredded Cheddar cheese
1½ cups milk	

Drain mushrooms, save liquid, add enough water to make 1 cup, set aside. Sauté onion in oleo, add flour and mustard. Cook over low heat until bubbly, stirring constantly. Stir in milk, mushroom liquid and bouillon cube. Cook until sauce thickens, boil 1 minute. Pour sauce over spaghetti; stir in mushrooms and ham. Put in 2-quart casserole. Sprinkle with cheese. Bake in 350° oven 45 minutes to 1 hour. Serves 6 to 8.

Rivertown Recipes

Pearl's Baked Country Ham
(Lard Stand Method—very old recipe)

16–22 pound country ham   2 cups sorghum
2 cups vinegar   Cold water to cover

Pour vinegar and sorghum over ham. Cover with water. Slowly bring to full boil. Boil for one hour.

Remove ham and container from stove and wrap tight in quilts or blankets. Let stand for 12 hours. Take ham out of water, cover with brown sugar and bake in medium oven—350°—until brown. Cool before slicing.

In the old days lard was bought in 10 gallon metal containers called "lard stands." When empty they were used for all sorts of things, cooking ham just being one of them. If you don't have a lard stand handy, use a large canner or any other pot with cover large enough to accommodate a 20-pound ham and enough water to cover.

Tennessee Treasure

Ham Mousse

HAM:

2 cups finely ground ham
½ cup sour cream
½ cup mayonnaise
½ cup heavy cream, whipped
1 tablespoon onion, grated

¾ cup Jezebel Sauce
¾ cup water
1 (¼-ounce) package unflavored gelatin
1 teaspoon salt

Sprinkle gelatin over cold water in saucepan. Place over low heat; stir until gelatin dissolves. Gradually add to sour cream and mayonnaise, stirring till smooth. Chill until slightly thickened. Stir in ham, onion, salt and Jezebel Sauce. Fold in whipped cream. Pour into 1-quart mold and chill until firm. Unmold and glaze with chaud-froid and decorate as desired.

CHAUD (Hot)-FROID (Cold) GLAZE:

2 (¼-ounce) envelopes unflavored gelatin
¾ cup chicken broth (canned)

2 tablespoons vinegar
2 cups mayonnaise

Combine chicken broth and vinegar in saucepan with gelatin. Place over low heat and stir constantly until gelatin is dissolved. With wire whisk, blend in mayonnaise until the mixture is very smooth. Pour ⅓ of this mixture over ham mousse and refrigerate until set (about 10 minutes). Reheat remaining glaze over very low heat until it liquefies. Pour ½ the remaining sauce over the mousse. Refrigerate mousse again. Repeat procedure with the remaining ⅓ of the glaze. Cover with plastic wrap and refrigerate until serving time. Serves 10–12 as an appetizer.

JEZEBEL SAUCE:

1 (16-ounce) jar pineapple preserves
1 (4-ounce) jar hot mustard

1 (16-ounce) jar apple jelly
1 (6-ounce) bottle horseradish
Salt and pepper to taste

Mix all ingredients in blender. Yields approximately three cups, and will keep in the refrigerator for months.

Southern Secrets

Liver & Lights Stew

This makes your tongue wag!

1 pound tripe	Boiling water
1 pound liver	1 skunk egg (onion)
1 pound heart	Salt and pepper to taste
1 pound brains	1 pod red pepper
¼ pound suet	2 tablespoons flour

Cut up all ingredients. Cover with boiling water. Season with onion, salt, pepper, and red pepper. Simmer over low heat 3 to 4 hours. Thicken with 2 tablespoons flour blended with cold water. This is so good!

Cracker Barrel Old Country Stores:
Old Timey Recipes & Proverbs to Live By

Opposum and Sweet Potatoes

1 opposum, scalded and cleaned*	1 tablespoon sugar
2 large sweet potatoes	Salt and pepper to taste
	Water

Parboil opposum in a large pot with enough water to cover. Let boil until tender. Place potatoes in separate pot with enough water to cover. Cook until done. Remove parboiled opposum from pot and place in a baking pan. Remove potatoes from pot, skin and slice. Place sliced potatoes around opposum. Add salt and pepper to opposum. Sprinkle sugar on top of potatoes. Cover. Place in 300° oven until slightly browned.

*Opposum may be cleaned by using scalding hot water until all fur is removed.

Our Favorite Recipes

Pluto Pups

12 frankfurters	1 teaspoon salt
12 wooden skewers	2 teaspoons sugar
½ cup flour	1 tablespoon baking powder
½ teaspoon sage	1 cup milk
½ cup cornmeal	2 eggs

Insert skewer in end of each frankfurter. Steam for 7 minutes. Cool. Sift dry ingredients together. Beat milk and eggs together and blend well into dry ingredients. Dip franks in batter and fry in deep fat at 350° until brown. Wrap handle in paper napkin. Serve at once.

Kountry Kooking

Seafood

White-water rafting on the Ocoee River, one of the finest white water rivers in the eastern United States.

Baked Stuffed Fish

3–4 pound fish
Flour, salt and pepper
Tomato juice
½ tablespoon melted butter
⅛ teaspoon salt

½ teaspoon onion juice
1 teaspoon chopped parsley
1 teaspoon capers or pickles

STUFFING:
¼ cup cracker crumbs

¼ cup stale bread crumbs

Mix all stuffing ingredients. Stuff into fish. Coat the outside of fish with flour, salt and pepper. Bake fish at 375° for 1 hour or until tender. Baste with tomato juice.

World's Fair Cookbook

Psari Plaki II
Baked Fish with Vegetables

3 pounds cod or haddock fillets
Salt and pepper

1 lemon, juice of

Season fish with salt, pepper and juice of lemon. Let stand.

SAUCE:
1 large onion, chopped
2 bunches green onions,
  chopped
5 tablespoons olive or vegetable
  oil
2 cloves garlic, minced
1 cup canned tomatoes

1 cup parsley, chopped
1 bell pepper, chopped
4 stalks celery, finely chopped
1 teaspoon salt
¼ teaspoon pepper
1 (8-ounce) can tomato sauce
½ cup white wine (optional)

Sauté onions in oil until soft; add garlic, tomatoes, parsley, bell pepper, celery and salt and pepper. Cook 10 minutes. Pour half of sauce in 9 × 13-inch baking dish; place fish on top and pour wine over fish. Cover with remaining sauce. Bake in oven at 350° for 45 minutes, basting often. Serve warm or cold. Yield: 6 servings.

It's Greek to Me!

Baked Fish with Shrimp–Parmesan Sauce

3 tablespoons butter
2 tablespoons flour
½ teaspoon salt
1 cup milk

2 pounds white fish fillets (ocean
   perch, flounder, sole, etc.)
½ pound small cooked shrimp
¼ cup Parmesan cheese, optional

Make a medium white sauce: melt butter in skillet, add flour and cook until bubbly, add salt and milk, stirring constantly. Remove from heat. Layer fish in a buttered flat baking dish. Spread shrimp and white sauce over fish. Sprinkle with Parmesan cheese. Bake for 20–25 minutes in a 325° oven.

Recipes from Miss Daisy's

Flounder Florentine

6 tablespoons butter
¼ cup minced onion
1 package cooked chopped
   spinach
¾ teaspoon marjoram leaves
½ teaspoon salt
¼ teaspoon pepper

2 pounds fillets
½ cup white wine
3 tablespoons flour
½ teaspoon dry mustard
1 cup milk
Parmesan, paprika, watercress

Melt 3 tablespoons butter in skillet. Add onion and sauté until tender. Stir in spinach, marjoram, ¼ teaspoon salt and ⅛ teaspoon pepper. Put 1½ tablespoons spinach mixture on each fillet and roll up. Put seam side down in baking dish. Add wine. Cover and bake 25 minutes at 350°. Drain and reserve ½ cup liquid. Keep fish warm. Melt remaining butter, add flour, salt, pepper and mustard. Add reserved liquid and milk. Stir until thick and boiling. Pour over fish. Sprinkle with Parmesan. Garnish with paprika and watercress.

Rivertown Recipes

Baked Flounder with Shrimp Sauce
A must for seafood lovers.

**8 flounder fillets (bass, trout, or
pompano may be substituted)**

Place each fillet on a piece of aluminum foil and spread each with shrimp sauce. Wrap so that no steam will escape. Bake at 350° for 45 minutes. Serve directly from foil.

SHRIMP SAUCE:

1¾ cups milk
3 tablespoons flour
1 cup butter or margarine
4 tablespoons chopped green
  pepper
1 tablespoon chopped pimento
½ cup chopped onion
1 teaspoon Worcestershire sauce

Dash red pepper
¾ teaspoon salt
½ garlic clove, minced
2 beaten egg yolks
¾ cup heavy cream
1½ cups chopped mushrooms
2½ pounds chopped, cooked
  shrimp

Using double boiler, make a thick sauce by melting butter and adding flour and milk. Then add green pepper, pimento, onion, Worcestershire sauce, red pepper, salt and garlic clove. Mix egg yolks and cream. Add to sauce. Then stir in mushrooms and shrimp. Yield: 8 servings.

Flaunting Our Finest

From the Mississippi River in the west to Lake Watouga high in the eastern mountains, Tennessee's 19,000 miles of streams and 29 major lakes offer some of the finest fishing and water recreation anywhere.

Poached Trout

This fish is poached on top of the stove in a large covered pan such as a frying pan with lid. It is a low-calorie, delicious protein food.

**1 rainbow trout large enough to
    serve 2 people**

POACHING WATER:

1 quart water   **½ teaspoon salt**
3 tablespoons vinegar   **¼ teaspoon dill weed**
1 shallot or green onion   **Peppercorns**

Place all ingredients for the poaching water into a pan large enough to hold the fish. Bring to boil.

Add the fish; cover. Turn down the heat on the stove; the fish should not be boiled. Poach it at just below simmer 4–7 minutes. Do not overcook. It should be juicy, not dry and flaky.

Hint: If cooking more fish, increase the amount of poaching water used.

More Home Cooking in a Hurry

Fish Pudding
(Calvary Church)

3 pounds red snapper or 3
  packages frozen fish
3 eggs
1 cup milk
1 stick butter, melted
½ cup cracker crumbs

1 tablespoon chopped parsley
1 tablespoon scraped onion
1 lemon
Sherry to taste
Salt to taste
Pepper

Fish should be baked with a little seasoning, boned and shredded. Then put in bowl, add eggs and beat in well. Add milk and ½ of butter, cracker crumbs, parsley, onion and lemon juice, sherry, salt and pepper. Put in baking dish and top with cracker crumbs and rest of butter. If mixture looks dry, add more milk. Set in pan of hot water and bake in 325° oven for 50 minutes. Serve with tartare sauce. Serves 8–10.

TARTARE SAUCE:

Take **1 cup stiff mayonnaise**, thin with **a little cream**. Add **chopped parsley, chopped sour pickle** and **capers**, if desired.

The Memphis Cookbook

Seafood Ragoût

1 pint oysters
¼ cup butter
¼ cup flour
¾ cup light cream
¾ cup thickly sliced mushrooms
2 pounds cooked shrimp
¾ cup cubed cooked chicken

Pinch cayenne pepper
Few drops onion juice
1½ teaspoons pepper
1 tablespoon parsley
¼ cup sherry
Salt

Parboil oysters in their own juice. Make a thick cream sauce with butter, flour, and cream. Add remaining ingredients. Pour into a 2-quart casserole and bake 30 minutes at 350°. Yield: 8 to 10 servings.

Nashville Seasons

Microwaved Bay Scallops in Cream Sauce

10 ounces bay scallops
1 small can evaporated milk
½ lemon
¾ stick margarine or butter
1 teaspoon parsley, dried

⅛ teaspoon paprika
⅛ teaspoon instant minced garlic
Pepper to taste
2 tablespoons flour
½ cup plain milk

Use 1-quart Pyrex dish and lid. Melt margarine and add to evaporated milk. Squeeze lemon and add juice. Combine parsley, paprika, garlic, and pepper; add to above mixture. Dissolve flour in milk, making sure no lumps remain; stir into above sauce. Add scallops and their juice; stir. Cover with lid and cook on high power in microwave 4–5 minutes, stirring at 2½ minutes. Sauce should thicken to a creamy consistency. Eat as a thick soup or serve over rice. Serves 2.

Koinonia Cooking

Salmon Croquettes

1 cup boned salmon
1 tablespoon butter
1 tablespoon flour
½ cup milk
1 teaspoon lemon juice

⅛ teaspoon pepper
½ teaspoon salt
Paprika
½ teaspoon black pepper

Make cream sauce with butter, flour, milk, salt and pepper, cooking until thick. Put salmon into bowl, add sauce and lemon juice; mix well with fork until salmon is well broken. Set aside; when cold, mold into desired shape, roll in bread crumbs, dip in egg beaten with 1 tablespoon cold milk, then in bread crumbs. Let dry an hour. Fry in deep hot fat. Serve with butter sauce.

Ground cooked chicken may be used instead of salmon.

Tennessee Treasure

Royal Seafood Casserole

1⅓ cups white long-grain rice, uncooked
2 cans condensed cream of shrimp soup
½ cup mayonnaise
1 small onion, grated
¾ cup milk
Salt
White pepper
Seasoned salt
Nutmeg
Cayenne pepper

3 pounds raw shrimp, cooked and cleaned
1 (7½-ounce) can crabmeat, drained
1 (5-ounce) can water chestnuts, drained and sliced
1½ cups chopped celery
3 tablespoons minced fresh parsley
Paprika
Slivered almonds for topping

Preheat oven to 350°. Cook rice until light and fluffy. Blend soup into mayonnaise in a large bowl. Stir until smooth. Add onion, then milk. Begin seasoning and use a heavy hand because the rice is bland and so is the seafood. When mixture is well seasoned, combine with shrimp, crabmeat, water chestnuts, celery, parsley, and rice.

Add additional salt, white pepper, seasoned salt, nutmeg and Cayenne pepper to taste. If mixture seems dry, add a few tablespoons milk, as mixture should be moist. Turn into a large shallow buttered casserole. Sprinkle with paprika and sprinkle almonds generously over the top. Bake uncovered for 30 minutes or until hot and bubbly. This freezes well. Serves 10.

Gazebo Gala

The homes of three U.S. Presidents, Andrew Jackson (The Hermitage), James K. Polk and Andrew Johnson are historic sights in Tennessee.

Shrimp Boil Dinner
With a salad, this is a complete meal.

2 packages crab boil
6 lemons, halved
1 tablespoon Tabasco sauce
2 to 3 tablespoons ice cream salt
20 new potatoes
15 onions, unpeeled
10 ears of corn, shucked and halved
6 pounds fresh, unpeeled shrimp

In a large roaster filled half full with water, bring the crab boil, lemon halves, Tabasco, and salt to a boil. Add the new potatoes and onions and boil until the potatoes are tender. Add corn. When corn is tender, add the shrimp. The shrimp is ready when it turns pink. This will take only a few minutes after the water has come to a full boil again. Drain and serve. Yield: 10 servings. Preparation time: 45 minutes.

Encore! Nashville

Hot and Spicy Barbequed Shrimp

3–4 pounds raw shrimp
½ teaspoon cayenne pepper
1 tablespoon thyme
½ teaspoon celery salt
1 tablespoon parsley, chopped
⅔ cup Worcestershire sauce
½ teaspoon black pepper
½ teaspoon salt
3 tablespoons olive oil
1 teaspoon crushed rosemary
½ pound butter

Combine all ingredients except shrimp. Heat until butter is melted and all ingredients are well blended. Marinate raw, unpeeled shrimp for at least 4 hours. (Cool marinade slightly before pouring over shrimp; marinate at room temperature 45 minutes, then refrigerate for remainder of time. Turn shrimp occasionally.) Bake, uncovered, at 350° for about 30 minutes, until shrimp are pink and firm. This is MESSY, but super. Serve lots of French bread to absorb the butter sauce.

Grand Tour Collection

Baked Shrimp

½ cup grated onion
4 tablespoons butter
½ pound grated Cheddar cheese
½ teaspoon dry mustard
½ teaspoon salt

½ teaspoon crushed garlic
1 pound cooked shrimp
6 tablespoons sherry
Grated coconut

Simmer onion in butter; add other ingredients except shrimp, sherry and coconut. Stir until cheese has melted; add sherry, pour over shrimp arranged in individual ramekins. Broil for 5 minutes under low heat; when almost done sprinkle with grated coconut and let brown. Serve very hot. Serves 6.

Woman's Exchange Cookbook I

Stir-Fry Shrimp Creole

1 pound shrimp, cleaned,
  deveined and boiled
1 large green pepper, cut into
  strips
1 large onion, sliced
1 cup fresh mushrooms, sliced
1 tablespoon cooking sherry
1 tablespoon soy sauce

1 tablespoon Worcestershire
  sauce
1 tablespoon butter or
  margarine
Pepper
Salt
1 (8-ounce) can tomato sauce

In a non-stick skillet, melt butter over medium heat. Sauté vegetables until tender with sherry, soy sauce, Worcestershire sauce and pepper. A dash of salt may be added, but be careful not to oversalt. Add shrimp and tomato sauce, stir lightly over low heat being careful not to break shrimp. Cook long enough to heat shrimp through but do not overcook. Serve over hot fluffy rice or alone.

Tennessee's 95 Magic Mixes: Second Helping

Bea's Artichoke-Shrimp Newburg

1 (9-ounce) package frozen artichoke hearts
1 bay leaf
1 (10¾-ounce) can cream of mushroom soup
2 tablespoons chopped onion
2 tablespoons white wine
½ teaspoon salt
⅛ teaspoon garlic salt
⅛ teaspoon pepper
1 pound cooked, peeled shrimp
½ cup grated Cheddar cheese

Cook artichoke hearts as directed, adding bay leaf during cooking. Drain. Combine soup, onion, wine, salt, garlic and pepper. Mix well. Arrange artichoke hearts and shrimp in casserole. Spread soup mixture over shrimp. Top with cheese and bake at 400° for 15 minutes. Serves 4.

Too easy to be so good.

Well Seasoned

Shrimp and Artichoke Casserole

1 (14-ounce) can artichoke hearts, drained
1½ pounds shrimp (boiled, shelled and deveined)
3 tablespoons butter or margarine
1 clove garlic, chopped
1 onion, or 4 green onions, chopped
¼ pound mushrooms, sliced, or 1 (4-ounce) can, drained
1 (10-ounce) can cream of mushroom soup
½ cup mayonnaise
1 tablespoon Worcestershire
2 tablespoons dry sherry
½ cup grated Parmesan cheese
1 (10-ounce) package frozen, chopped spinach, thawed and drained
Salt, paprika, and pepper to taste

Place artichokes in buttered 2-quart casserole. Add shrimp. Sauté garlic, onions and mushrooms in the butter. Add undiluted soup, mayonnaise. Worcestershire sauce, sherry, cheese, salt, and pepper. Add well-drained spinach (squeeze out water). Pour this mixture over shrimp. Sprinkle with more Parmesan cheese and paprika. Bake 20 minutes at 375° or until bubbly. May be garnished with chopped parsley or buttered bread crumbs. Serves 6.

Maury County Cookbook

Braised Shrimp with Vegetables

1 pound large fresh shrimp
8 ounces fresh broccoli
2 (4-ounce) cans button
  mushrooms
1 tablespoon vegetable oil
1 (8-ounce) can sliced bamboo
  shoots

½ cup chicken broth
1 teaspoon cornstarch
¼ teaspoon sugar
½ teaspoon ginger
⅛ teaspoon pepper

Shell and devein shrimp. Cut broccoli spears into pieces. Drain mushrooms. Heat oil in wok or skillet until hot. Stir-fry shrimp in oil until tender, for about 3 minutes. Add broccoli to shrimp and stir-fry for 1 minute. Add mushrooms and bamboo shoots; stir-fry for 1 minute. Combine chicken broth, cornstarch, sugar, ginger and pepper and pour over shrimp and vegetable mixture. Cook and stir until liquid boils. Cook and stir 1 minute longer. Serve over rice. Yield: 4 servings.

Out of this World

Dee's Shrimp Spaghetti

1 (12-ounce) package vermicelli
  spaghetti
1 pound shrimp, cooked,
  cleaned, cut into bite-size
  pieces
1 (6-ounce) can sliced
  mushrooms, drained
¾ cup margarine, melted

8 ounces shredded Cheddar
  cheese
¼ cup grated Parmesan cheese
1 tablespoon plus 1 teaspoon
  garlic powder (adjust to taste)
Salt to taste
Cracked pepper to taste

In large saucepan, break spaghetti in half and cook according to package directions. While spaghetti is cooking, prepare remaining ingredients so they can be added immediately. Drain spaghetti and put back in saucepan. Add remaining ingredients. Toss like salad until cheese is melted. Serve immediately. Note: this is even better the next day.

Dixie Delights

Shrimp and Wild Rice Casserole

1 stick butter	3 cans mushroom soup
1 pound box wild rice	1½ soup cans water
1 large onion, chopped	1 tablespoon salt

Sauté rice and onion in butter and then add 3 cans mushroom soup and 1½ soup cans of water and 1 tablespoon salt. Place in casserole and cook in oven 1 hour covered at 325°. Add more water if dry. Then add:

1½ pounds cooked shrimp	1 (8-ounce) package fresh
1 large green pepper, chopped	mushrooms, undrained (stems
1 can water chestnuts, chopped	and pieces)

Return to oven about 30 minutes. Chicken can be used in place of shrimp.

Grand Tour Collection

Crabmeat Patties

This is a great recipe for crabcakes. The reason I think it is good is that this is about the way we have been making patties by ear for years. The bread crumbs and eggs seem to form a better base than the thick white sauce that some recipes call for.

Mix these ingredients:
1 pound crabmeat   **2 eggs**
2 cups soft bread crumbs

Blend:
1 teaspoon dry mustard   **½ teaspoon each salt and pepper**
1 teaspoon Worcestershire sauce   **¼ teaspoon Tabasco**
2 tablespoons lemon juice   **4 tablespoons melted butter**
1 tablespoon vinegar

Blend all seasonings. Add to crab mixture. Divide into 8 patties. Roll in flour. Beat 1 egg and thin with a little milk. Dip patties in egg-and-milk mixture and then in cracker meal. Chill about 1 hour before cooking. Drop each patty in hot fat (350°) and brown.

Chattanooga Cook Book

Crabmeat Au Gratin

1 tablespoon plus 1 teaspoon all-purpose flour
½ cup butter
1½ cups Half and Half
1 tablespoon plus 1 teaspoon chopped green onion
1 tablespoon plus 1 teaspoon chopped parsley
1½ cups sharp Cheddar cheese, grated
⅛ teaspoon Tabasco sauce
Salt and pepper to taste
1 pound lump crabmeat (fresh)

In a double boiler, make a white sauce with flour, butter and cream. Add onion and one tablespoon parsley. Add one cup cheese and seasonings. Carefully stir in crabmeat. Pour into a buttered casserole; top with remaining cheese and bread crumbs. Bake at 350 for 25 minutes or until hot and golden brown. Remove from oven and sprinkle with remaining parsley. Serves 4 to 6.

Palate Pleasers

Crab Meat Mousse

2 pounds crab meat
2 cup finely chopped celery
1 bottle capers, drained
1 cup chopped olives
2 cups mayonnaise
2 tablespoons Worcestershire
2 tablespoons dry mustard
2 teaspoons vinegar
4 envelopes gelatin
1 cup cold water
1 cup heated milk
Lemon juice to taste

Mix crab meat, celery, capers and olives. Stir in mayonnaise. In a separate bowl, mix Worcestershire and mustard; then dissolve in vinegar. Soften gelatin in cold water and add to hot milk. Combine all ingredients, adding lemon juice to taste. Pour into 2-quart greased mold. If done in a ring mold, center of mold can be filled with mashed avocado seasoned with lime or lemon juice. Serves 12.

Party Potpourri

Broiled Crab Melt-a-Ways

⅓ cup margarine
2 tablespoons mayonnaise
½ teaspoon seasoned salt
½ teaspoon garlic salt
1 (7-ounce) jar sharp Cheddar
  spread

1 (6-ounce) package frozen
  crabmeat, thawed and drained
  or 1 (7-ounce) can, rinsed and
  drained
6 English muffins

Mix all ingredients, except English muffins. Split muffins and spread with mixture. Cut into fourths. Put on cookie sheet (may be frozen at this point). Broil until golden brown when ready to serve. Yield: 12 to 16 servings.

Flaunting Our Finest

Quiche,
Pasta,
Rice

The Parthenon in Nashville is the only full-scaled exact replica of the ancient temple in Athens, Greece.

Mushroom Pie

2 pounds fresh mushrooms	1½ cups chicken stock
6 tablespoons butter	½ cup Madeira wine
Salt and pepper	½ cup heavy cream
Juice ½ lemon	1 pie dough
3 tablespoons flour	1 egg, beaten

Wash, dry and trim mushrooms. Reserve the stems for another use. In a large skillet heat 4 tablespoons butter, add mushrooms, sprinkle with salt, pepper, and lemon juice. Cover, cook 10 minutes, shaking pan frequently. Arrange mushrooms in buttered 1-quart baking dish piling them high in the center. To the juices remaining in the pan, add 2 more tablespoons butter. Stir in flour. Gradually add chicken stock and cook, stirring constantly, until sauce is smooth and thickened. Stir in wine and hot cream, season with salt and freshly ground pepper. Pour sauce over the mushrooms, cover with flaky pie dough. Brush with beaten egg. Make a few slits in the top and bake for 15 minutes at 450°. Reduce heat to moderate and bake for 10–15 minutes longer. Serves 8.

This is simply marvelous, especially served with roast beef.

Woman's Exchange Cookbook I

Mushroom Quiche

1 (9-inch) pie shell	4 eggs, beaten
2 tablespoons oil	1 cup milk
½ large onion, chopped	1 teaspoon basil
½ cup fresh mushrooms	½ teaspoon marjoram
1 cup shredded cheese (Cheddar, Swiss)	½ teaspoon salt
	1 green pepper slice
4 ounces cream cheese	

Bake pie crust at 450° for 5 minutes. Place oil in skillet on medium heat. Add onions and mushrooms. Sprinkle onion and mushrooms in bottom of pie shell. Cover with grated cheese. Combine softened cream cheese with other ingredients. Beat smooth and pour into shell. Place green pepper slice on top. Bake at 450° for 10 minutes and reduce to 375° for 35 minutes.

Tennessee Homecoming: Famous Parties, People & Places

Cheese Pie (Unbaked)

1 cup saltine cracker crumbs
(about 24)
3 tablespoons margarine, melted
8 ounces cream cheese, at room
temperature
½ cup chopped celery
½ cup chopped pitted black
olives (about 16 large)
¼ cup chopped red bell pepper
(or drained canned pimento
peppers if red peppers are not
available)

1 cup sour cream
½ cup chopped green bell pepper
1 tablespoon snipped chives
(may use freeze dried)
1 tablespoon Worcestershire
sauce
3 or 4 drops hot pepper sauce
(optional)
½ teaspoon salt
Garnish: chopped ripe black
olives or fresh spinach leaves

Lightly butter bottom and sides of an 8-inch spring form pan. Mix crumbs and melted butter until blended. Press over bottom of pan; refrigerate until chilled and firm.

Stir cream cheese in medium-size bowl until smooth. Add remaining ingredients (except garnish). Stir until blended. Spoon over crust; spread well (but leave rough looking). Cover with plastic wrap or foil; refrigerate for several hours. To serve, run tip of a knife around edge of pan. Gently loosen and remove sides of pan. Leave pie on pan base, place on a serving plate. Garnish and serve.

Maury County Cookbook

Pizza on Rye

1 pound ground beef
1 pound mild sausage
1 pound Velveeta cheese,
chopped
1 teaspoon basil

1 teaspoon oregano
1 teaspoon garlic powder
2 tablespoons parsley flakes
1½ loaves party rye bread

Brown meats together and drain well. Return to heat and add cheese. Let melt, then add rest of ingredients except bread. Spoon onto slices of bread. Place on a cookie sheet and freeze. Do not thaw. When ready to serve, broil 5 to 7 minutes and serve hot.

Great with soups or salads.

Well Seasoned

Macaroni Mousse

1 cup elbow macaroni, uncooked
1 pimento, chopped
1 bell pepper, chopped
1 tablespoon chopped parsley
1 tablespoon chopped onion
½ teaspoon salt
Dash of red pepper
½ cup margarine
3 eggs
2 slices loaf bread, cut into small cubes
1½ cups grated sharp Cheddar cheese
1½ cups milk

Heat oven to 350°. Butter a 1½-quart baking dish. Cook macaroni according to directions on package. Mix pimento, pepper, parsley, onion, salt, red pepper and margarine together with macaroni. Beat eggs slightly, pour over bread cubes. Add 1¼ cups of cheese. Combine with macaroni mixture. Place in prepared dish. Pour the milk over this and top with remaining ¼ cup cheese.

Can be prepared several hours or day before and refrigerated until an hour before cooking time. Serves 6–8.

Palate Pleasers

Macaroni and Cheese

8 ounces elbow macaroni, cooked and drained
1 can mushroom soup
1 cup mayonnaise (Hellmann's)
¼ cup pimento, chopped
⅓ cup onion
1 pound sharp cheese, grated
1 cup mushrooms
Cheese Ritz crackers

Mix all ingredients. Crumble cheese Ritz on top. Heat in 400° oven for 15–20 minutes and serve immediately. Freezes well (before cooking).

Rivertown Recipes

Cheese-Noodle Casserole
A nice accompaniment to meat dishes.

4 ounces broad noodles
1 cup sour cream
1 cup cottage cheese
1 egg, lightly beaten
1 small onion, chopped fine
⅛ teaspoon garlic powder
  (optional)

1 teaspoon Worcestershire sauce
½ teaspoon salt
¼ teaspoon pepper
Extra sour cream (optional)
Chopped chives (optional)
Grated Parmesan cheese
  (optional)

Cook noodles as directed on package, until barely tender. Drain and rinse. Combine sour cream, cottage cheese, egg, onion, seasonings, and noodles. Turn into a buttered 1½-quart baking dish. (Buttered ring mold may be used.) Sprinkle with Parmesan cheese. Bake at 325° for about 1 hour. Serve with additional sour cream, chives, or grated Parmesan. Serve 6.

If baked in a mold, ring may be turned onto platter and filled with colorful buttered vegetables of choice.

The Nashville Cookbook

Easy Rice Casserole

1 cup Uncle Ben's long grain
   rice
1 medium can sliced mushrooms
   (do not drain)

1 can French onion soup
1 can sliced water chestnuts
⅔ stick butter

Mix all ingredients. Top with butter pats and bake uncovered for 1 hour at 350°.

Palate Pleasers

Mushroom-Pecan Rice

1 cup uncooked rice
½ teaspoon nutmeg
1 can mushroom soup
Small can mushroom stems and
  pieces

3 ounces pecan or almond pieces
½ cup butter, melted

Cook rice, rinse, and season with nutmeg. In a well-greased casserole, layer rice, undiluted mushroom soup, mushrooms and nuts. Repeat layers, ending with nuts on top. Pour melted butter over all. Bake for 20 minutes at 350°. Serves 6–8.

Party Potpourri

Mexican Grits

2 cups quick grits
½ pound grated sharp Cheddar
  cheese
½ cup butter or margarine
2 teaspoons Tabasco
½ teaspoon salt

2 cloves garlic, crushed
3 eggs, beaten
1 can green chiles, chopped
2 jalapeño peppers, seeded and
  chopped

Cook grits as directed. Mix in cheese, making sure cheese melts thoroughly, butter, Tabasco, salt, garlic, eggs, chiles and jalapeno peppers. Pour mixture into greased casserole and bake at 350° for 45 minutes. Serves 10.

Kiss My Grits

24 Hour Wine and Cheese Casserole

½ large loaf day-old French
  bread, broken into small pieces
3 tablespoons unsalted butter,
  melted
½ pound Swiss cheese, shredded
¼ pound Monterey Jack cheese,
  shredded (reserve ½ cup)
5 thin slices baked ham, coarsley
  chopped

8 eggs
1½ plus ⅛ cups milk
¼ cup white wine
2 large onions, grated
1 tablespoon German mustard
⅛ teaspoon black pepper
1/16 teaspoon red pepper
¾ cup sour cream
½ cup grated Parmesan cheese

Grease (spray) a 9 × 13-inch Pyrex baking dish. Spread bread in bottom and drizzle with melted butter. Sprinkle on Swiss and Monterey Jack cheese and ham.

Beat together eggs, milk, wine, grated onion, mustard and peppers until foamy. Pour over cheese and other ingredients. Cover with foil and refrigerate overnight.

Preheat oven 30 minutes at 325°. Bake covered until set, about 1 hour, uncover and spread with sour cream; sprinkle top with Parmesan and remainder of shredded cheese. Bake at 350° uncovered until crusty and brown, about 10–15 minutes.

Palate Pleasers

Vegetables

A peaceful farm in the valley of the Smoky Mountains. Beneath Mt. Leconte.

Sautéed Tomatoes

3 tomatoes, peeled and
   quartered
2 tablespoons butter
1 tablespoon cooking oil
1 clove garlic, mashed
½ teaspoon salt
Pepper to taste

½ teaspoon sugar
1 tablespoon lemon juice
2 tablespoons green onion,
   chopped
2 tablespoons parsley, chopped
2 tablespoons basil, chopped

If using dried parsley and basil, use only one tablespoon each. Heat
fat on medium; add other ingredients. Sauté 2–3 minutes. Serves 4.

Home Cooking in a Hurry

Microwave Spinach and Tomatoes

1 (10-ounce) package frozen
   spinach, chopped
¾ cup ricotta cheese, drained
½ teaspoon garlic powder
¼ teaspoon nutmeg

Salt and pepper, to taste
2 tomatoes, thinly sliced
½–¾ cup mozzarella cheese,
   grated
Parmesan cheese

Defrost spinach and drain to remove all liquid. Mix with ricotta
cheese, garlic, nutmeg, salt and pepper. Spread half of mixture in
bottom of 1-quart casserole. Cover with half of tomato slices and
sprinkle with half of mozzarella cheese. Repeat layers; sprinkle top
with Parmesan cheese. Cover with wax paper and cook on medium
power in microwave until cheese is melted is heated thoroughly,
approximately 8–10 minutes. *May be baked in conventional oven at
350° for 20 minutes.* Yield: 6 servings.

Upper Crust: A Slice of the South

Spinach Stuffed Tomatoes

3 strips bacon
¼ cup chopped onion
½ pound fresh spinach, snipped
½ cup sour cream

4 medium tomatoes
Salt
½ cup shredded mozzarella
    cheese

Cook bacon until crisp; drain, reserving 2 tablespoons drippings. Crumble bacon and set aside. Cook onion in reserved drippings until tender; stir in spinach. Cook, covered, until tender, 3 to 5 minutes. Remove from heat; stir in sour cream and bacon. Cut tops from tomatoes; remove centers, leaving shells. Drain on paper towels. Salt shells, then fill with spinach mixture. Place in an 8 × 8-inch baking pan and bake for 20 to 25 minutes at 375°. Top with shredded cheese and bake for 2 or 3 minutes more, until cheese is melted.

Note: This is an elegant accompaniment, especially good with a beef entree. Yield: 4 servings.

Out of this World

Spinach and Tomato Bake

4 medium tomatoes
1 (10-ounce) package frozen
    chopped spinach, thawed and
    well drained
½ cup herb stuffing mix

1 tablespoon chopped onion
1 egg, beaten
¼ cup butter, melted
¼ cup Parmesan cheese

Slice each tomato into 2 thick slices. Let drain if they should be watery. Place in a greased baking dish in a single layer, sliced side facing up. Place remaining ingredients in a bowl and mix well. Make mounds of the spinach mixture on each tomato slice. Bake for 15 minutes in a 350° oven.

Recipes from Miss Daisy's

Spinach Madeleine

2 (10-ounce) packages frozen
  chopped spinach
4 tablespoons butter
2 tablespoons flour
2 tablespoons chopped onion
½ cup evaporated milk
½ cup vegetable liquor

½ teaspoon black pepper
¾ teaspoon celery salt
¾ teaspoon garlic salt
Salt to taste
1 (6-ounce) roll Jalapeño cheese
1 teaspoon Worcestershire
Red pepper to taste

Cook spinach according to directions on package. Drain and reserve liquor. Melt butter in saucepan over low heat. Add flour,
stirring until blended and smooth, but not brown. Add onion and
cook until soft, but not brown. Add liquid slowly, stirring constantly to avoid lumps. Cook until smooth and thick; continue
stirring. Add seasonings and cheese which has been cut into small
pieces. Stir until melted. Combine with cooked spinach. This may
be served immediately or put into a casserole and topped with
buttered bread crumbs. The flavor is improved if the latter is done
and kept in refrigerator overnight. This may also be frozen. Serves
5 to 6. This can be used as a dip and is very good. Heat in a
saucepan and put in chafing dish. Serves 20.

Southern Secrets

Noodle-Spinach Ring

2 packages frozen, chopped
  spinach
8 ounces noodles
1 onion, chopped

½ stick oleo
Salt and pepper
1 cup sour cream
3 eggs, slightly beaten

Cook spinach and set aside. Cook noodles according to package
directions. Sauté onion in butter. Then mix all of the ingredients
together. Season with salt and pepper. Pour into a well-greased ring
mold and place in a shallow pan with water in the bottom. Cook at
350° for 45 minutes. Unmold on platter, surround with parsley and
sprinkle generously with freshly grated Parmesan cheese.

This would be wonderful to serve in place of a baked potato with
steak, duck, chicken—or anything!

A Man's Taste

Spinach-Artichoke Casserole

1 (6-ounce) can whole
   mushrooms, drained
1 (6-ounce) can mushroom
   pieces, drained
6 tablespoons butter
1 tablespoon flour

½ cup milk
1 teaspoon salt
Dash pepper
2 (10-ounce) packages frozen,
   chopped spinach, cooked

Sauté mushrooms in butter. Remove and separate whole crown and pieces. Add flour to melted butter left and cook until bubbly. Add milk, stir until smooth. Add salt, pepper, mushroom pieces, and spinach. Drain artichokes. Place in casserole and cover with spinach mixture. Pour sour cream sauce over casserole and top with whole mushrooms. Bake in 350° oven about 30 minutes. Serves 8.

SOUR CREAM SAUCE:
½ cup sour cream   ½ cup mayonnaise
2 tablespoons lemon juice

Blend ingredients. Heat and pour on casserole.
   Note: This can be frozen, but do not freeze with sour cream sauce.

NCJW Cookbook

Baked Stuffed Squash

10 medium yellow squash
¾ cup shredded sharp Cheddar
  cheese
1 small onion, finely chopped
⅛ teaspoon salt
⅛ teaspoon pepper
2 tablespoons butter

¼ teaspoon dry mustard
⅛ teaspoon curry powder
1½ teaspoons Worcestershire
  sauce
⅛ teaspoon Tabasco sauce
½ cup cracker cumbs
⅛ teaspoon paprika

Cook squash in salted water until tender. Select 8 of uniform size and scoop out centers, reserving shells. Mash centers with remaining squash, removing any coarse seeds. Add the cheese, onion, salt, pepper, butter, mustard, curry powder, Worcestershire sauce, and Tabasco sauce. Stuff mixture into shells and sprinkle with cracker crumbs and paprika. Place into a $12 \times 8 \times 2$-inch glass baking dish with a small amount of water and bake for 30 minutes at 325°. Yield: 8 servings.

Nashville Seasons

Green and Gold Squash

1 medium onion, chopped
2 tablespoons salad oil
¾ pound zucchini, shredded
  coarsely
¾ pound yellow squash,
  shredded coarsely
2 tablespoons chopped parsley

½ teaspoon salt
½ teaspoon basil
¼ teaspoon pepper
3 eggs, slightly beaten
½ cup milk
1 cup shredded sharp cheese
½ cup saltine crumbs

In large frying pan, sauté onion in oil until golden. Remove from heat. Stir in next 6 ingredients. Add eggs and milk. Spoon ½ of mixture in 1½-quart casserole. Sprinkle with ½ of cheese and ½ of crumbs. Repeat. Bake, uncovered, at 325° for 45 minutes.

Dixie Delights

My Zucchini Squash

This is a great recipe. If you prefer to use canned tomatoes instead of V-8 juice, it takes a little longer to cook. I use V-8 juice because of the different seasonings, which add to the flavor of the zucchini. This dish is best suited to people who like Italian seasonings. It's hard to say how much oregano to use—I like oregano, so I use a lot.

4–5 green onions, chopped
2 tablespoons butter or
  margarine
3 large zucchini
Salt and pepper

Oregano
V-8 juice
1 teaspoon brown sugar
  (optional)

In heavy skillet or Dutch oven with lid, sauté green onions in butter until clear and tender. Wash zucchini. Do not peel. Slice crossways. Place in skillet with sautéed onions. Sprinkle with salt, pepper and oregano. Pour V-8 juice over zucchini until well covered. Add brown sugar, if desired. Put top on Dutch oven or skillet. Cook slowly over low heat until zucchini is very tender. Makes 6 servings.

Minnie Pearl Cooks

Squash Casserole
Delicious!

1 pound yellow crookneck
  squash
1 small onion
Salt and pepper to taste
1 cup grated sharp cheese

¼ cup butter
3 eggs, separated
½ cup milk
10 saltine crackers

Cut squash and onions and cook together until tender, using as little water as possible. Drain and mash well. Add salt and pepper, cheese, butter, egg yolks, milk and crumbled up crackers.

Beat egg whites very stiff and fold into mixture. Cook in greased casserole dish until brown, about 30 minutes, at 350°.

Sam Houston Schoolhouse Cookbook

Eggplant Casserole

1 medium eggplant	1 egg, slightly beaten
1 pound ground beef	Dash of pepper
½ cup onion, chopped	1 cup sharp cheese, grated
¼ cup green pepper, chopped	1 can French-fried onion rings
1 can tomatoes, chopped	¼ cup butter

Peel and slice eggplant. Cook until tender in boiling salted water. Drain and mash with fork. Brown ground beef and drain. Mix eggplant, ground beef, onion, green pepper, tomatoes, egg and pepper. Layer eggplant mixture, cheese and fried onion rings, ending with onion rings on top. Dot with butter. Bake in a greased casserole pan at 350° for 30 to 40 minutes. Serves 6 to 8.

Elvis Fans Cookbook II

Mousaka I
Eggplant Casserole

2 pounds ground beef (very lean)
1 cup chopped onion
1 clove garlic, finely chopped
½ stick butter
1½ teaspoons salt
1 teaspoon black pepper
1 cinnamon stick
1 bay leaf
¼ cup chopped parsley
1 (8-ounce) can tomato sauce
1 cup water
3 eggs
2 large eggplants (fried potato slices may be combined with eggplant)
1 cup grated Parmesan cheese

Brown meat with onion, garlic, butter, salt, pepper, cinnamon stick and bay leaf. Add parsley, tomato sauce, water; simmer until meat is done and mixture thickens (about 30 minutes). Set aside to cool. When meat has cooled, remove cinnamon stick and bay leaf. Add 3 beaten eggs to mixture.

Slice eggplants into round ½-inch thick slices. Soak for 15 minutes in salted water. Drain thoroughly and blot with paper towel. Fry slices in hot vegetable oil until light brown. Drain on paper towel. (Hint: Cover several sheets of newspaper with paper towel, lay eggplant slices in single layer, cover with more paper towel, blot.)

CREMA SAUCE:
3 cups milk
6 tablespoons butter
6 tablespoons flour
6 eggs, beaten
¼ cup grated Parmesan cheese
½ teaspoon salt
¼ teaspoon pepper

Heat 2 cups milk to scalding, add butter, remove from heat. Blend flour into 1 cup cold milk. Stir cold mixture into hot mixture. Return to heat, stirring constantly until thickened. Remove from heat and add eggs, cheese, salt and pepper.

Sprinkle bottom of $11 \times 15 \times 2$-inch baking pan with ¼ of cheese; place a layer of eggplant, sprinkle with ¼ of cheese; place meat sauce, cover with layer of eggplant, sprinkle with ¼ of cheese; top with Crema Sauce and sprinkle with remaining ¼ of cheese; and bake at 350° until golden brown. Yield: 24–28 servings.

It's Greek to Me!

Marinated Green Beans

4 slices bacon	½ cup vinegar
½ cup sugar	1 (16-ounce) can cut green beans

Brown bacon in pan, remove and set aside. Add sugar and vinegar to bacon grease and stir. Add green beans. Simmer about 20 minutes. Then add crumbled bacon and simmer about 5 minutes.

Note: This is always a favorite. I usually double it. Yield: 4 servings.

Flaunting Our Finest

Greenbean Casserole

DRAIN WELL AND LAYER:

1 (16-ounce) can French-style greenbeans	1 (8-ounce) can water chestnuts, washed, drained, sliced
1 (16-ounce) can white shoe peg corn	

MIX TOGETHER FOURTH LAYER:

1 (10¾-ounce) can cream of celery soup	½ cup sour cream
	½ cup chopped onion

ADD FIFTH AND SIXTH LAYERS:

1 cup shredded Cheddar cheese
1 stick melted butter mixed with
   1 pack crushed Ritz crackers
   and garlic powder to taste

Sprinkle sliced almonds on top. Bake at 350° for 30 to 40 minutes. (Glass dish 325°.)

Gatlinburg Recipe Collection

Southern Green Beans

2 pounds tender pole beans
3–4 ounces slab bacon (cured
  without smoke)
2 teaspoons salt

1 tablespoon molasses
  (sorghum)
2 cups water
Black pepper to taste

Wash beans; remove tip ends and strings; break in 2-inch lengths. Cut bacon in ¼-inch slices and place in bottom of large heavy pan. Sauté over medium heat until slices appear to be clear but not brown. Put beans in pan; add salt and enough water to cover (about 2 cups). Bring to a boil over high heat; cover and reduce to medium-low heat. Cook for 20 minutes. Add molasses, stir, cover, and cook for 1 hour or until most of water is evaporated. At this stage the beans will be tender but firm. If you prefer a wilted texture, simmer 1 hour longer. Add more salt, if needed, and serve with sprinkling of freshly ground black pepper. Serves 6.

Variations: (1) Steam small new potatoes on top of beans during last 30 minutes of cooking time. (2) Steam small onions or quartered large onions. (3) Steam small tender okra pods on top of beans for 25–20 minutes. (4) A very small pod of fresh (green) hot pepper may be cooked with the beans.

The James K. Polk Cookbook

Marinated Green Peas

1 (16-ounce) can green peas
1 clove garlic, minced
¼ teaspoon celery seed
¼ cup lemon juice

⅓ cup salad oil
Dash pepper
¼ teaspoon salt

Drain peas. Place liquid in pan; add other ingredients except peas. Bring fluid to a boil; add peas. Remove from heat; chill. Serve cold. Makes 4 servings.

More Home Cooking in a Hurry

Vegetables Parmigiana

2 tablespoons olive oil
1 eggplant, peeled and sliced
2 zucchini, sliced
1 green pepper, cut in squares
2 large onions, sliced
½-1 pound mozzarella cheese, sliced

2 cups tomato sauce
½ teaspoon salt
⅛ teaspoon pepper
¼ teaspoon oregano
2–3 tablespoons grated sharp cheese

Heat oil in large skillet; add eggplant, zucchini, green pepper and onions. Cook until barely tender. Layer ½ vegetables, cheese and sauce in greased baking dish, seasoning layers with salt, pepper and oregano. Repeat. Sprinkle with grated sharp cheese. Bake at 350° for 20–30 minutes, or until cheese is melted. Serves 6–8.

Great meatless main dish!

Well Seasoned

Broccoli-Cheese Casserole

2 packages frozen chopped
  broccoli
4 tablespoons butter
½ cup chopped celery, optional

½ cup chopped onion, optional
1 can mushroom soup
1 roll bacon or garlic cheese

Cook broccoli according to directions on package; drain well. Melt butter in skillet; sauté celery and onion, if desired. Stir in soup and cheese until melted and well blended; add broccoli. Pour into greased casserole. Top with bread crumbs, cracker crumbs, or onion rings, if desired. Bake at 350° for 20 minutes.

Koinonia Cooking

Broccoli Puff with Curried Mayonnaise

1 (10-ounce) package frozen
  broccoli spears
3 tablespoons butter
3 tablespoons flour
1 teaspoon salt

1 cup milk
⅛ teaspoon nutmeg
1 teaspoon lemon juice
4 eggs, separated

Cook broccoli according to package directions, drain, and chop finely. Melt butter, add flour and salt and cook until bubbly. Add milk. When thick, add nutmeg, lemon juice, and broccoli. Cool slightly and add beaten egg yolks. Cool mixture completely and fold in stiffly beaten egg whites. Pour into buttered 1½-quart soufflé dish. Place dish in pan containing 1 inch of hot water and bake at 325° for 1 hour. Mix together topping ingredients and serve with casserole. Serves 6.

TOPPING:
½ cup sour cream
½ cup Hellmann's mayonnaise

¼ teaspoon curry powder

Well Seasoned

French Fried Cauliflower

1 box frozen cauliflower
2 eggs

Bread crumbs (sifted)

Parboil cauliflower until barely tender. Drain well. Dip in beaten eggs and bread crumbs and fry until brown. Serves 4.

Smoky Mountain Magic

Snow Peas and Mushrooms

1–2 tablespoons cooking oil
2 cups fresh snow peas
1 cup sliced fresh mushrooms
3–4 green onions, sliced (or 1
   small white)

2 teaspoons soy sauce
¼ cup water

Place oil in wok or frying pan; heat on medium-high. Add all the vegetables. Stir-fry 1 minute.

Reduce heat to medium and add soy sauce and water. Cook 1 or 2 more minutes. Serves 3 or 4.

More Home Cooking in a Hurry

Baked Asparagus

1 (16-ounce) can asparagus or 2
   cups fresh cut into 1-inch
   lengths
2 hard cooked eggs, sliced

½ cup slivered almonds
½ pound Cheddar cheese, grated
1 can cream of mushroom soup
1 cup Ritz cracker crumbs

Preheat oven to 350°. Layer drained asparagus, eggs, almonds and cheese in greased baking dish; cover with soup. Sprinkle with crumbs. Bake for 35 minutes until thick and bubbly. Yield: 4–5 servings.

Miss Daisy Entertains

Celery Casserole

4 cups celery, diced
1 large can water chestnuts,
  drained and sliced
2 cups cream sauce
1 (8-ounce) package cream
  cheese

Salt to taste
Dash Worcestershire sauce
1 chopped onion
Dash of Tabasco

Cook celery in water to cover until tender, about 15 minutes. Drain and add water chestnuts. Stir in remaining ingredients. A good side dish. Can be put in a Pyrex dish and reheated the next day.

Note: If you are looking for something a little different to serve, this is a good choice.

Parties & Pleasures

Celery Almondine

½ cup slivered almonds
4 tablespoons butter, divided
4 cups celery, diagonally sliced
1 tablespoon onion, minced

Salt, pepper and seasoned salt, to
  taste
2 tablespoons dry white wine

Sauté almonds in 1 tablespoon butter. Remove and reserve almonds. Melt remaining butter; add celery, onion and seasonings. Cook over low heat, stirring occasionally for about 10 minutes. Add almonds and wine. Cook until almonds are reheated. This can be made ahead, except for adding almonds and wine. Yield: 4–6 servings.

Children like it too!

Upper Crust: A Slice of the South

Lorene's Kraut Recipe
(She's used it for 50 years)

Cabbage
Salt

Sugar
White vinegar

Cut cabbage and pack in quart fruit jars. Add to each quart 1 teaspoon salt and 1 teaspoon sugar; then to each quart add 1 tablespoon white vinegar. Fill jar with water and seal. (Lorene prefers the lids with rubber rings.)

Cookin' & Quiltin'

Red Cabbage
(Rotkohl)

2 tablespoons cooking oil
2 small onions, sliced
2 pounds red cabbage, shredded
3 tablespoons vinegar
Salt to taste
2 teaspoons sugar

1 large tart apple, peeled, cored, and finely chopped, or ½ cup applesauce
½ cup red wine
½ cup beef broth

Heat oil in a Dutch oven and sauté onions 3 minutes. Add cabbage and immediately pour vinegar over cabbage to prevent it from losing its red color. Sprinkle with salt and sugar. Add chopped apple or applesauce. Pour in red wine and beef broth. Cover and simmer for 45 minutes. Makes 4 servings.

Das Germantown Kochbuch

Hopping John

1 cup dry black-eyed peas	1 clove garlic, minced
8 cups water	1 cup regular rice
6 slices bacon	2 teaspoons salt
¾ cup chopped onion	¼ teaspoon pepper

Rinse the black-eyed peas. In a large saucepan combine the peas and water, bring to a boil, then boil for 2 minutes. Remove from heat and let stand 1 hour. Drain, reserving 6 cups of the cooking liquid.

In a heavy 3-quart saucepan, cook the bacon, onion, and garlic until the bacon is crisp and the onion is tender but not brown. Remove bacon; drain on paper towels; crumble and set aside.

Stir the black-eyed peas, raw rice, salt, pepper, and the reserved cooking liquid into mixture in saucepan. Bring to a boil; cover and reduce heat. Simmer 1 hour, stirring occasionally. Stir in crumbled bacon. Turn into a serving bowl. Serve immediately. Makes 8 servings.

Tennessee Treasure

Ellen Smith's Bean Casserole

8 bacon slices	1 (15-ounce) can butter beans
4 onions, sliced and ringed	1 (15-ounce) can lima beans
1 cup brown sugar	1 (15-ounce) can dark red
½ cup vinegar	kidney beans
1 teaspoon dry mustard	1 (11-ounce) can Morton's
½ teaspoon salt	baked beans
½ teaspoon garlic powder	1 (15-ounce) can cut green beans

Fry bacon until crisp and drain. Cook onions in bacon drippings until clear. Add brown sugar, vinegar, mustard, salt, garlic powder and simmer for 20 minutes. Drain cans of beans well and combine with onions and spices. Pour mixture in 3-quart casserole dish and bake in 350° oven until hot. Do not overcook or beans will be mushy. Crumble bacon on top before serving. Serves 8 to 10.

Southern Secrets

Deluxe Baked Beans

1 pound ground beef
1 large onion, chopped
1 bell pepper, chopped
1 stick margarine
¾ cup ketchup
¾ cup brown sugar

16 ounces tomato sauce
1 tablespoon liquid smoke
1 tablespoon Worcestershire
3 cups kidney beans
1 can mushrooms
1 cup cheese, grated

Sauté meat, onion, and pepper in margarine. Add ketchup, sugar, tomato sauce, liquid smoke and Worcestershire sauce. Lastly, add beans, mushrooms and grated cheese. Bake, covered, at 350° for 1 hour.

Joyce's Favorite Recipes

Baked Beans

2 (16-ounce) cans baked beans
3 tablespoons onion, grated
3 tablespoons celery, chopped
3 tablespoons brown sugar
3 tablespoons dark molasses
3 tablespoons vinegar

3 tablespoons catsup or chili sauce
2 teaspoons mustard
⅛ teaspoon salt
⅛ teaspoon pepper
4 strips of bacon

Mix all ingredients together except bacon. Place into a 2-quart casserole, cover with strips of bacon, and bake for 2 hours at 325°.

Note: The flavor is improved if the beans are mixed several hours before baking. Yield: 8 servings.

Nashville Seasons

Beets with Orange Sauce

⅓ cup sugar
2 tablespoons cornstarch
⅛ teaspoon salt

1 cup orange juice
1 tablespoon butter
3 cups cooked diced beets

Combine dry ingredients; add orange juice and butter. Cook for 5 minutes in top of double boiler or over very low heat in heavy saucepan. Add beets and let stand for several hours before serving. Serve very hot. Yield: 6–8 servings.

Miss Daisy Entertains

Carrot–Raisin Casserole

⅓ cup soft butter
½ cup sugar
3 eggs, beaten
3 cups cooked, mashed carrots

¾ cup raisins
¾ cup milk
¾ teaspoon baking powder
Grated rind of 1 lemon

Cream butter and sugar. Add eggs and mix. Blend in remaining ingredients. Bake in a buttered casserole for 30 minutes in a 350° oven.

Recipes from Miss Daisy's

Carrot Casserole

2 cups mashed cooked carrots
   (8–12 depending on size)
½ cup margarine
1 cup sugar

3 tablespoons flour
1 teaspoon baking powder
3 eggs, beaten
1 teaspoon pumpkin pie spice

Add margarine to hot carrots and stir until melted. Stir in remaining ingredients. Bake in a buttered casserole dish for 15 minutes at 400°. Reduce heat to 350° and bake an additional 30 to 45 minutes or until lightly browned.

I usually make one-third of this recipe and it takes only 20 minutes at 350° after 15 minutes at 400°. Serves 6.

St. Paul Cooks

Corn Pudding Tennessee Style
It's creamy and delicious

2 cups corn (fresh or canned)
4 tablespoons flour
2 level teaspoons sugar
1 level teaspoon salt

2 well beaten eggs
2 tablespoons butter, melted
2 cups milk

Mix corn, flour, sugar and salt. Combine well-beaten eggs, melted butter and milk. Mix with corn mixture. Pour into greased baking dish. Bake at 350° for 1 hour. Stir from bottom 2 or 3 times the first 30 minutes of baking. Double recipe for 12.

Tennessee Homecoming: Famous Parties, People & Places

Corn Casserole Supreme

1 (17-ounce) can cream-style
    corn
2 eggs, beaten
½ cup crushed soda crackers
¼ cup margarine, melted
¼ cup undiluted evaporated
    milk
¼ cup finely shredded carrots

1 teaspoon chopped onion
¼ cup chopped green pepper
¼ cup chopped celery
1 teaspoon Tabasco sauce
½ teaspoon sugar
Salt
½ cup grated Cheddar cheese
Paprika

Combine corn and all ingredients except cheese and paprika. Mix thoroughly and turn into greased 8 × 11-inch baking dish. Top with cheese. Sprinkle with paprika. Bake at 350° for 30 minutes. Serves 8 generously.

I like it baked in deeper round casserole.

The James K. Polk Cookbook

Tennessee Fried Corn

Cream style fresh roastin' ears, not really fried,
but so called by most middle Tennesseans.

2 cups (6 to 8 ears) fresh corn
5 tablespoons butter and bacon
  drippings, mixed
1 teaspoon sugar

Salt and pepper to taste
½–¾ cup water for each cup
  corn

Select corn with full round, milky kernels. Remove shucks and silks. Cut tips of kernels from ears of corn; scrape with edge of knife to remove all of milky portion remaining on cob. Heat fat in skillet. Add corn, seasonings, and water, stirring constantly for about 2 minutes to heat through. Lower heat and cook, stirring frequently, until corn is thickened and color almost transparent (about 15–20 minutes). Serves 4–6.

The Nashville Cookbook

Fresh Corn and Tomato Casserole

8–12 ears fresh corn
¼ cup butter or bacon drippings
2 cups water
4 slices crisp bacon, crumbled

1 teaspoon salt or to taste
2 large tomatoes, peeled and
  sliced

Cut corn from cob. There should be 4 to 5 cups of cut corn. Melt butter or drippings in skillet, add corn, and sauté quickly for about 5 minutes. Add water, bacon and salt and pour in buttered casserole. Arrange sliced tomatoes on top. Place in a moderate oven (350°) and bake uncovered about 30 minutes. Serve hot; 5 to 6 servings.

Tennessee Treasure

Fresh Corn au Gratin

3 tablespoons butter
1 tablespoon flour
½ cup milk
½ cup grated mild Cheddar
   cheese

3 cups fresh or frozen corn
1 teaspoon ground nutmeg
1 teaspoon salt
¼ teaspoon white pepper
½ cup Ritz cracker crumbs

Preheat oven to 350°. Melt 1 tablespoon butter in saucepan; blend in flour. Stir in milk; cook until medium thick, stirring constantly. Add cheese, corn, nutmeg, salt and pepper; mix well. Turn into buttered casserole. Melt remaining butter and mix with cracker crumbs. Sprinkle over casserole. Bake for 35 to 40 minutes or until crumbs are brown. Yield: 5–6 servings.

Miss Daisy Entertains

Creamed Hominy

Creamed hominy we originally got from Fannie Warren, one of the most famous cateresses Chattanooga has ever had. She helped us with a large brunch once and she promised that it would be the best thing we had. She was right. She put it in a heavy pan with cream and butter and let it cook gently for an hour until the cream had cooked down and was thick. To this day we have been doing hominy this way for buffets.

2 (15-ounce) cans white hominy
½ cup whipping cream
½ stick butter

Salt and pepper
Dash of Tabasco
Chopped parsley

Get two cans of white hominy and drain off the liquid. Put it in a heavy saucepan. Pour in ½ cup whipping cream and ½ stick butter, a little salt and pepper and a dash of Tabasco. This must simmer slowly for about an hour until the cream has turned to a thick sauce. For a large group double or triple the recipe, since this recipe will serve about 6 or 8 persons.

Before serving, butter a round mixing bowl. Pack the hominy into this. Unmold onto a platter and sprinkle the top with chopped parsley.

Chattanooga Cook Book

Creamed Potatoes–My Mother's Way

2–2½ pounds potatoes   1 cup milk
1 stick margarine   Salt to taste

Peel and slice potatoes ½-inch thick. Put in large saucepan and cover with water. Boil at medium heat for about 20 minutes or until potatoes are tender enough to stick a fork into. (Careful about overcooking). Drain water off potatoes. Place potatoes in electric mix bowl. Add margarine and salt. Beat on mixer until margarine is melted. Meanwhile, scald the milk in same saucepan potatoes were cooked in. Do not boil milk. Add milk to potatoes. Whip until all lumps are gone. To keep warm for serving, put potatoes back in saucepan and set in pan of water over very low heat. I have lots of requests for this recipe.

Family Favorites by the Miller's Daughers

Harriet's Potatoes

Time and time again Harriet would come by for a visit, stop beside my herb garden, ask if she could have some parsley, and announce she was going to fix the potatoes her family liked. I don't know why it took me at least a year to ask her for that recipe for those potatoes they enjoyed so much.

8 medium potatoes, boiled   1 teaspoon celery salt
1½ cups mayonnaise   ½ teaspoon salt
1 cup sour cream   1 medium onion, grated
1½ teaspoons prepared   Fresh parsley, chopped
   horseradish   Paprika

Boil potatoes in skin, peel and slice into thin rounds. Make sauce of remaining ingredients except parsley and paprika. In flat casserole dish, layer sliced potatoes and sauce, ending with sauce. Top with finely chopped fresh parsley and dust with paprika. Cover and refrigerate several hours to allow the flavors to blend.

. . . and garnish with Memories

Cheese Potatoes

8–10 large potatoes, cooked and
  diced
1 stick butter
1 cup sour cream

1 roll garlic cheese
Salt and pepper to taste
1 cup Cheddar cheese, grated

Dice potatoes and cook until tender, drain. Add butter to potatoes, add sour cream. Cut up roll of garlic cheese and add to other ingredients. Add salt and pepper. Top with grated cheddar cheese. Bake at 350° for 25 minutes. Serves 8.

Palate Pleasers

Potato Soufflé

3 tablespoons butter
3 tablespoons all-purpose flour
1 cup light cream
1 teaspoon minced onion

1 cup mashed potatoes
3 eggs, separated
Salt and pepper

Melt butter and blend in flour. Add cream and cook, stirring, until thickened. Add onion and potatoes; heat, stirring until hot. Stir in beaten egg yolks quickly. Season, and fold in stiffly beaten egg whites. Spoon into 1½-quart soufflé dish, and bake in preheated moderate oven for 30 minutes, until puffed and firm. Makes 4 to 6 servings.

World's Fair Cookbook

Potato Casserole

2 cups cream style cottage cheese
1 cup sour cream
12 cups sliced green onions
1 small clove garlic (optional)
2 teaspoons salt

5 cups cooked potatoes diced
½ cup shredded American
  Processed Cheese
Paprika

Combine first 5 ingredients. Fold in potatoes and pour into greased 1½-quart flat casserole. Top with cheese and paprika. Bake in 350° oven 40 minutes.

Rivertown Recipes

Velveeta Potatoes

12 medium potatoes, cooked
 with skins on
1 teaspoon salt
1 cup chopped onion
½ chopped green pepper

1 pound Velveeta cheese, cubed
3 slices buttered bread, cut into
 cubes
1 cup melted butter

Cook, cool and peel potatoes. Butter a 13 × 9-inch baking dish. Dice potatoes and place in dish. Add salt, onion, green pepper and cheese cubes. Place buttered bread cubes over all and pour on melted butter. Sprinkle with 2–3 teaspoons parsley. Bake at 350° for 1 hour.

Elvis Fans Cookbook

Sweet Potato Casserole

6 medium sweet potatoes, grated
½ stick butter, melted
3 eggs, separated
½ cup sugar
1 teaspoon ginger

1 teaspoon nutmeg
Grated rind of 1 orange
½ cup molasses
½ teaspoon salt

Mix all ingredients except egg whites, stirring until well blended. Fold in stiffly beaten egg whites and bake in greased casserole in moderate oven for 20–30 minutes.

The Memphis Cookbook

Reba McEntire's Praline Sweet Potato Casserole

1 large can sweet potatoes
   (drained)
¼ teaspoon salt
1 teaspoon vanilla

½ teaspoon cinnamon
⅓ cup sugar
¼ cup melted oleo
2 eggs

Mash potatoes, add other ingredients, put in greased casserole.

TOPPING:
¼ cup melted oleo
3 tablespoons flour

¾ cup brown sugar
½ cup pecans (chopped)

Mix and sprinkle over top of potato mixture. Bake at 350° for 30 minutes.

Reba McEntire, *Elvis Fans Cookbook II*

Southern Okra

1 cup cut okra	1 tablespoon sugar
1 chopped green pepper (sweet)	1 teaspoon flour
1 chopped onion	½ teaspoon pepper
¼ cup oil	½ teaspoon salt
3 tomatoes peeled and quartered	

Cook okra in boiling salted water for 10 minutes and drain. Brown onion and pepper in oil. Add tomatoes and cook 5 minutes. Add other ingredients and cook until done while stirring (about 10–15 minutes).

Palate Pleasers

Baked Stuffed Onions

These may be made the day before, refrigerated, and baked before serving.

6 large onions, peeled	¼ cup chopped pecans
3 tablespoons butter or margarine	Salt and pepper
¼ cup dry bread crumbs	1½ cups grated sharp cheese
	Paprika

Choose onions that are uniform in size. Cook in boiling salted water for about 25 to 30 minutes or until tender, but not soft. Drain and cool.

Carefully scoop out centers. Chop and sauté in butter until golden. Cool. Add bread crumbs, pecans, salt, pepper, and part of the cheese. (Save enough cheese to sprinkle on top.) When ready to bake, preheat oven to 350°. Grease shallow baking dish. Place onions in baking dish. Top with remaining cheese. Sprinkle with paprika. Bake about 15 minutes, or until cheese is melted and slightly brown. Makes 6 servings.

Minnie Pearl Cooks

Mrs. Guerry's Baked Apricots

2 large cans apricot halves
Butter
Brown sugar

Cinnamon
Ritz crackers, crumbled

Butter the bottom of a baking dish. You will need two large cans of apricot halves. Drain the fruit, reserving the liquid for later if necessary. Place 1 can apricot halves in a baking dish and dot each half with butter. Sprinkle with brown sugar and a little cinnamon. Top this with a layer of crumbled Ritz crackers.

Repeat this whole process again so that you have two layers of apricots. Top the whole casserole with plenty of Ritz crumbs and butter. You probably won't need to add any juice, but add a small amount if you need to. The casserole should be moist and delicious but not runny. Bake for half hour or 45 minutes in a 375° oven.

Chattanooga Cook Book

Broiled Grapefruit

½ grapefruit per serving

Brown sugar

Slice grapefruit in half; cut out center, remove seeds; run knife around edge to loosen membrane. Sprinkle brown sugar on top. Broil until sugar melts. Serve warm with cherry in center.

Home Cooking in a Hurry

Hot Fruit Casserole

1 package dried pitted prunes
Ground cinnamon
1 package dried apricots
1 large can pineapple chunks,
  drained

2 small cans mandarin oranges,
  drained
1 (25-ounce) jar Musselman's
  cherry pie filling

Place prunes in Pyrex casserole and sprinkle with cinnamon. Layer, and sprinkle with cinnamon, apricots, pineapple chunks, mandarin oranges and cherry pie filling. Bake in pre-heated oven at 325° for 30 or 40 minutes. Keeps well.

The Original Tennessee Homecoming Cookbook

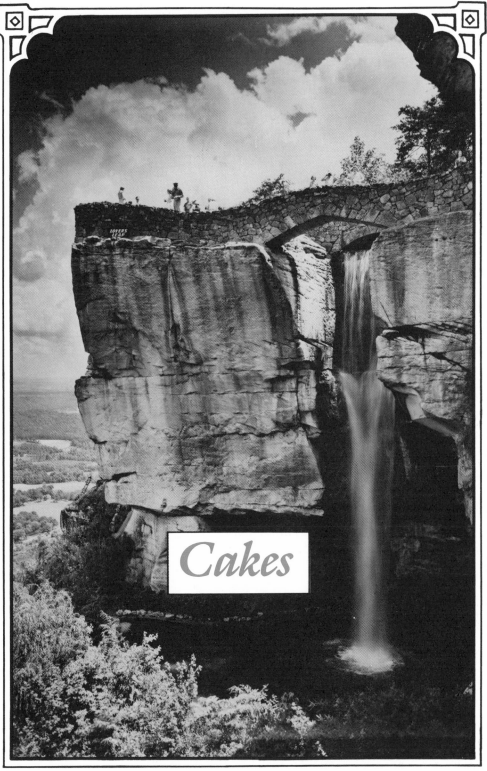

Cakes

Lovers Leap in Beautiful Rock City. Near Chattanooga.

Nashville's One-Pan Fudge Cake

½ cup butter
1 cup sugar
1¼ ounces bittersweet chocolate
½ cup flour
¼ teaspoon baking powder

2 eggs
1 teaspoon vanilla
1 cup nuts, broken
⅛ teaspoon salt

Melt butter, sugar, and chocolate together. Sift flour and baking powder into the same bowl. Add eggs, vanilla, nuts, and salt. Blend and pour into a well greased 8-inch square pan. Bake at 325° for 35 minutes. Cut into squares while hot, but do not remove from pan until cooled. Yield: 1 dozen.

Nashville Seasons

Chocolate Sheet Cake

1¼ cups butter
½ cup cocoa
1 cup water
2 cups flour (plain)
1½ cups packed brown sugar
1 teaspoon soda
1 teaspoon cinnamon

½ teaspoon salt
1 can Eagle Brand milk
2 eggs
1 teaspoon vanilla
1 cup confectioners' sugar
1 cup chopped nuts

Preheat oven to 350°. Melt 1 cup butter; stir in ¼ cup cocoa, then water. Bring to a boil, remove from heat. In a large mixing bowl, combine flour, brown sugar, soda, cinnamon and salt. Add cocoa mixture; beat well. Stir in ⅓ cup Eagle Brand milk, eggs and vanilla. Pour into greased jelly roll pan. Bake for 15 minutes. In a small saucepan, melt remaining ¼ cup butter. Add ¼ cup cocoa and Eagle Brand milk. Stir in powdered sugar and nuts. Spread on warm cake.

St. Paul Cooks

Burning Love Chocolate Cream Cake

3 squares unsweetened chocolate
2¼ cups sifted flour
2 teaspoons baking soda
½ teaspoon salt
½ cup butter or margarine,
  softened
2¼ cups firmly packed light
  brown sugar

3 eggs
1½ teaspoons vanilla
1 cup dairy sour cream
1 cup boiling water
Whipped Cocoa Cream

Melt chocolate in a small bowl over hot (not boiling) water and cool. Grease and flour two (9 × 1½ inch) pans. Tap out excess flour.

Sift flour, baking soda and salt onto waxed paper. Preheat oven to 350°. Beat butter, sugar and eggs in a large bowl with electric mixer on high speed until light and fluffy. Beat in vanilla and cooled chocolate. Stir in dry ingredients, alternating with sour cream and beating well with a spoon until smooth. Stir in water. (Batter will be thin.) Pour into pans. Bake for 35 minutes or until centers spring back when lightly pressed with fingertips. Cool in pans 10 minutes, then turn on wire racks and cool completely. Split each layer in half crosswise to make 4 thin layers. Fill and frost with Whipped Cocoa Cream. Refrigerate.

WHIPPED COCOA CREAM:
⅔ cup confectioners' sugar
1 teaspoon vanilla

1 pint heavy cream
½ cup unsweetened cocoa
  powder

Whip ingredients in a medium bowl until stiff.

Elvis Fans Cookbook II

Beale Street in Memphis is the birth place of the blues. Memphis musicians include W. C. Handy, Jerry Lee Lewis, Charlie Rich, B. B. King, Al Green, and Elvis Presley.

Chocolate Cherry Cake

1 package devil's food cake mix
1 (21-ounce) can cherry pie
  filling

1 teaspoon almond extract
2 eggs, beaten

Preheat oven to 350°. Grease and flour 9 × 13 × 2-inch pan. In large bowl, combine all ingredients and mix well. Bake 25 to 30 minutes and frost while warm.

FROSTING:
1 cup sugar
5 tablespoons margarine
⅓ cup milk

1 (6-ounce) package semi-sweet
  chocolate chips

In small saucepan, combine first 3 ingredients. Cook until it comes to a boil, stirring constantly. Stir one minute longer. Remove from heat. Add chips. Stir until smooth.

Dixie Delights

Chocolate Fudge Upside Down Cake

¾ cup sugar
1 tablespoon butter
½ cup milk
1 cup all-purpose flour
½ teaspoon salt
1 teaspoon baking powder

1½ tablespoons cocoa
½ cup chopped pecans
½ cup sugar
½ cup brown sugar
¼ cup cocoa
1¼ cups boiling water

Cream together sugar and butter. Add milk. Stir well. Sift together flour, salt, baking powder and cocoa. Add to milk mixture. Stir well. Pour into greased 9-inch round cake pan. Sprinkle with chopped nuts. Mix together sugar, brown sugar and cocoa. Sprinkle over top of dough and nuts in pan. Pour boiling water over all. Do not stir. Bake at 350° for 30 to 40 minutes. Let cool in pan. Cut in wedge pieces. Turn upside down to serve, spooning sauce over top. Serve with ice cream. Yield: 8 servings.

Dixie Delights

Chocolate Torte

1½ sticks margarine
2 cups plain flour
1 cup finely chopped nuts
8 ounces cream cheese
1 cup powdered sugar

1 large carton Cool Whip
2 small packages instant
   chocolate pudding
3 cups milk

Melt margarine. Mix together flour, margarine, and nuts; press into 9 × 13-inch pan. Bake at 350° about 25 minutes or until brown. Cool. Mix cream cheese and powdered sugar; beat until fluffy. Stir in 1 cup Cool Whip. Spread over crust. Mix chocolate pudding with milk. Beat until thick; spread over cheese layer. Spread remainder of Cool Whip over top; sprinkle with nuts.

Koinonia Cooking

Chocolate Yule Log

On the screened porch, which is the best refrigerator at Christmas, is our Christmas dessert, the Chocolate Yule Log. I first saw this as an illustration in the "Gourmet Cookbook," a Mother's Day present long ago. It was beautiful . . . a light chocolate roll filled with whipped cream and iced with mocha icing. The garnishes of icing from the pastry tube, the little chocolate twigs, the nuts on top make this so spectacular looking that we use it all year round . . . a Lincoln log in February and chocolate log when we have twelve for dinner and need one dessert that will feed that many.

I have changed the recipe so that it scarcely resembles the original, but it is quickly made and a great favorite. For grownups, we sometimes flavor the icing with rum or brandy but our children don't like it, so at Christmas we just use the chocolate and coffee flavors. Don't let the long recipe scare you. One night Susan and I had to make six and had a fresh one in the oven every twenty minutes.

6 egg whites	**1 teaspoon vanilla**
¼ teaspoon cream of tartar	**¼ cup cocoa**
½ cup sugar	**¼ cup flour**
6 egg yolks	**½ teaspoon salt**
½ cup sugar	

Beat the egg whites with the cream of tartar until stiff. Gradually add the ½ cup sugar and beat until stiff and glossy. In another bowl beat the egg yolks and gradually add the ½ cup sugar. Put in the vanilla. Sift dry ingredients and quickly fold into the yolk mixture. Fold in the egg whites.

Take a long cookie pan, about 10 × 15 inches, and fit into it a piece of foil. Grease the foil with oil. Pour in the batter and bake at 325° for 20 to 25 minutes. When done, turn out on cup towel, peel off foil, and roll up while warm just as you would jelly roll. Let cool all rolled up.

WHIPPED CREAM FILLING:

2 cups whipping cream	**1 teaspoon sugar**

First chill the beaters and small bowl of mixer in the freezer. This makes the cream whip faster and to a smoother texture. Whip the cream and sweeten it. Set aside to wait in the refrigerator until time to fill the roll.

CONTINUED

CONTINUED

MOCHA ICING:

1 teaspoon instant coffee
3 tablespoons water (or rum or brandy)
3 cups sifted powdered sugar

1 tablespoon cocoa, sifted
Pinch of salt
¼ cup butter

Melt the instant coffee in the water. Sift the cocoa with the sugar. Blend all together in the mixer until fluffy. You may have to add more sugar to get the right consistency.

Unroll the chocolate roll and remove to a platter. Fill with the whipped cream and roll up again. Ice with the icing. If you want to, cut off one slice of the roll and break into three pieces. Roll up each of these to make mock twigs to garnish the iced roll. It is pretty, but not necessary to put some of the icing in a paper cone and run through a large star pastry tube to decorate the edges of the roll. Do sprinkle chopped pecans on the top.

Chattanooga Cook Book

Apricot Nectar Cake

1 large package yellow cake mix
1 (3-ounce) box lemon Jello
¾ cup apricot nectar
1 tablespoon lemon extract

4 egg yolks
4 egg whites
¾ cup Wesson oil

GLAZE:

2 cups confectioners' sugar

2 lemons

In large mixing bowl, combine cake mix and Jello. Add remaining ingredients except egg whites. Mix well on medium speed. Fold in stiffly beaten egg whites and pour into tube pan. Bake at 325° for 1 hour. Remove from oven. Leave cake in pan and pour over it a mixture of 2 cups confectioners' sugar and juice of 2 lemons. After pouring mixture over cake, allow to cool completely before removing from pan.

St. Paul Cooks

100-Year Old Clove Cake

1 cup margarine (2 sticks)	1 tablespoon cinnamon
2¼ cups sugar	¼ teaspoon salt
5 eggs	1 teaspoon baking soda
3 cups sifted flour	1 cup sour milk
1 tablespoon cloves	

Soften margarine. Gradually add sugar and cream well. Beat eggs thoroughly in a separate bowl. Add to sugar mixture and beat until light. Sift dry ingredients together and add ⅓ at a time to batter. Add ½ cup sour milk and another ⅓ of dry ingredients; mix well. Stir soda into remaining milk and mix into batter with remaining flour. Bake in well-greased and floured 10-inch tube pan at 350° for 45–55 minutes or until cake pulls away from side of pan. Cool 10 minutes. Remove to cake rack and cool thoroughly.

This cake is the one used by Mrs. Teddy Roosevelt. Does not need frosting, it's so good.

Our Favorite Recipes

Pistachio Cake

1 yellow cake mix	3 eggs
½ cup nuts	½ cup cooking oil
1 package instant pistachio pudding	1 cup Club Soda (Canada Dry)

Mix all except soda. Add this last. Bake at 350° for 40–45 minutes.

TOPPING:

1 pint whipping cream	1 package instant pistachio pudding
1 cup milk	

Beat together and frost cake.

Elvis Fans Cookbook

Apricot Almond Cakes

½ cup butter
½ cup sugar
1 teaspoon almond extract
1 egg

1½ cups flour
1 teaspoon baking powder
½ cup ground almonds
Apricot jam

Cream together butter and sugar. Add almond extract and egg. Beat well; then fold in mixture of flour, baking powder and ground almonds. Work to stiff paste. Press ½ of mixture into greased 8-inch layer pan and spread thinly with apricot jam. Spread remainder of mixture over jam. Bake 30 minutes in 350° oven. Cool and cut into 16 (2-inch) squares.

Party Potpourri

Black Bottom Cupcakes

1 (8-ounce) package cream
  cheese, softened
1 egg
⅓ cup sugar
⅛ teaspoon salt
1 (6-ounce) package semi-sweet
  chocolate chips
1½ cups flour
1 cup sugar

¼ cup cocoa
1 teaspoon soda
½ teaspoon salt
1 cup water
1⅓ cups cooking oil
1 tablespoon vinegar
1 teaspoon vanilla
Sugar
Chopped nuts

Combine first four ingredients; beat well. Add chocolate chips. In a separate bowl sift together flour, sugar, cocoa, soda and salt. Add to flour mixture: water, oil, vinegar and vanilla. Beat until well blended. Fill muffin tins, lined with paper baking cups, ⅓ full of chocolate batter. Top each with a heaping teaspoon of cream cheese mixture. Sprinkle with sugar and chopped nuts. Bake at 350° for 25 to 30 minutes. Do not overbake. Makes 24.

Woman's Exchange Cookbook II

Tennessee Jam Cake

¾ cup butter or margarine,
  softened
1 cup sugar
½ teaspoon vanilla
3 eggs
1½ cups self-rising flour
¼ teaspoon soda
½ teaspoon cinnamon
½ teaspoon ground cloves
½ teaspoon allspice
¼ cup buttermilk
½ cup strawberry preserves
½ cup blackberries, drained
1 cup plum jelly

Heat oven to 325°. Grease and flour 2 (8-inch) cake pans. Cream butter, sugar and vanilla. Add eggs, flour, soda, cinnamon, cloves, allspice. Stir in buttermilk, strawberry preserves and blackberries. Save plum jelly for spreading between layers. Bake until tested done, about 30–35 minutes. Cool in pans about 10 minutes; then remove to cake rack to cool. When cake layers are completely cool, move to cake plate and spread plum jelly between the layers. Frost with Caramel Frosting.

CARAMEL FROSTING:

¾ cup butter or margarine
2 cups dark brown sugar, packed
½ cup evaporated milk
1 teaspoon vanilla
3 cups powdered sugar

Cook butter, brown sugar and milk in heavy saucepan to almost soft ball stage, or about 210° on candy thermometer. Remove from heat. Add vanilla and stir in powdered sugar gradually until the frosting becomes a good spreading consistency. Frosts 2 (8-inch) layers.

Maury County Cookbook

Strawberry Jam Cake

1 cup butter
2 cups sugar
4 eggs
1 teaspoon soda
1 cup buttermilk
1 teaspoon cinnamon

3 cups flour
1 teaspoon salt
1 teaspoon cloves
1 teaspoon allspice
1½ cups strawberry jam
1 teaspoon vanilla

Cream butter and sugar, add eggs. Dissolve soda in buttermilk and mix alternately with the dry ingredients. Add jam and vanilla. Makes two 10-inch pans or three 8-inch pans. Bake in 350° oven for 45 minutes or less for the 8-inch pans.

Parties & Pleasures

The deepest river gorge in the South is on the Nolichunky River. And Fall Creek Falls (256 feet) is one of the highest waterfalls in America.

Somersault Cake

"Put fo' tablespoons er butter in a iron skillet, and when it melts up, add a ginerous cup er brown sugar. Pat it down smooth. Now sprinkle a cup er diced pineapple an a cup er pecans and a cup er raisins. Now po a cup of honey over this, a dribblin hit around.

Now po' in yer favorite cake mix batter—white, yellow, spice or ginger.

Bake in a 350° oven for 35 minutes. Turn out on plate before hit sets up.

Serve it up with whipped cream. This'll sho' make 'em foller they noses back ter the kitchen." (As sent to me!—Granny Nanny.)

Kountry Kooking

Orange Rum Cake

4 well-beaten eggs
1 box deluxe yellow cake mix
1 cup water
1 (3-ounce) box lemon instant
   pudding mix
½ cup salad oil

Add all ingredients to well beaten eggs. Beat until well blended. Pour into greased and floured 10-inch tube pan. Bake at 325° about 1 hour, or until center springs back when touched lightly. While cake bakes, mix:

⅓ cup orange juice
⅓ cup rum
⅔ cup sugar

Let stand to dissolve sugar. When cake is done, instead of removing from pan, run knife around sides and center of pan. While cake is hot, drizzle mixture over entire cake. Make at least 1 day before serving and store in pan, covered with plastic wrap, until ready to serve. This is the cake that is served most often at our house. This cake freezes real well.

Family Favorites by the Miller's Daughters

Italian Cream Cake

½ cup shortening
½ cup margarine
2 cups sugar
5 eggs, separated
2 cups flour
1 cup buttermilk

Dash of salt
1 teaspoon baking soda
1 teaspoon vanilla
1 cup pecans, chopped
½ cup coconut

Save egg whites. Cream shortening, margarine, sugar, and egg yolks until fluffy. Set aside. Mix flour, buttermilk, salt, soda, and vanilla and set aside. Beat egg whites until stiff and fold into butter milk/flour mixture. Combine the two and add pecans and coconut. Mix well. Pour into greased/floured 3 × 9-inch pan and bake 30–40 minutes at 350°. Top with icing recommended below.

ICING:
1 stick margarine
8 ounces cream cheese
1 box powdered sugar

1 teaspoon vanilla
1 cup pecans, chopped

Cream margarine and cheese; then add powdered sugar, vanilla, and pecans, mixing well after each addition.

Joyce's Favorite Recipes

Dreamy Coconut Cake
Tastes as if it were made from scratch!

1 (18½-ounce) box white cake mix
1 can Eagle Brand milk
1 (9-ounce) carton non-dairy whipped topping

1 (8½-ounce) can cream of coconut
1 (6-ounce) package frozen coconut, thawed

Grease a 13 × 9-inch baking pan. Bake cake according to package directions. While cake is still hot, punch holes in the top with a fork or straw and pour milk over entire top; cool. Mix whipped topping and cream of coconut together by hand and spread over cake. Top with coconut.

Out of this World

Pumpkin Cake

½ cup shortening
1 cup sugar
1 cup brown sugar, firmly
  packed
2 eggs, beaten
1 cup cooked, mashed pumpkin
  or winter squash

3 cups sifted cake flour
4 teaspoons baking powder
¼ teaspoon baking soda
½ cup milk
1 cup walnuts, chopped
1 teaspoon maple extract

Cream shortening and slowly add sugars, eggs and pumpkin. Sift together flour, baking powder and soda; add alternately with milk to mixture. Fold in walnuts and extract. Pour into 3 greased 8-inch layer cake pans. Bake at 350° for 30 minutes. Cool and frost with Harvest Moon Frosting.

HARVEST MOON FROSTING:

3 egg whites, unbeaten
1½ cups brown sugar, firmly
  packed

Dash of salt
6 tablespoons water
1 teaspoon vanilla

Combine in double boiler eggs, sugar, salt and water. Beat well; place over rapidly boiling water. Cook 7 minutes, beating constantly, or until frosting will stand in peaks. Remove from boiling water; add vanilla. Beat until thick enough to spread. Put cake layers together with frosting. Frost sides, bringing frosting slightly over top edge. Frost top. Makes enough frosting for a 3-layer cake.

Cookin' & Quiltin'

Pineapple Cake

1 can sweetened condensed milk	10 maraschino cherries, sliced
¼ cup lemon juice	½ cup heavy cream, whipped
10 marshmallows, quartered	Lady fingers
½ cup crushed pineapple	

Combine condensed milk and lemon juice and stir until thickened. Add marshmallows, pineapple, cherries and whipped cream. Line a 9-inch spring form pan with lady fingers. Stand halves around the outer edges of pan; pour in filling with care. Cover top with lady fingers. Chill in refrigerator overnight.

Tennessee Homecoming: Famous Parties, People & Places

Quick Apricot Crunch Cake

1 (1-pound 6-ounce) can apricot pie filling	⅓ cup water
1 small box white cake mix	½ cup flaked coconut
1 egg	½ cup chopped pecans
1 teaspoon almond extract	½ cup butter, melted
	Whipped cream

Preheat oven to 350°. Spread pie filling in 9-inch square pan. Beat cake mix, egg, extract and ⅓ cup water for 4 minutes. Pour over filling. Sprinkle with coconut and pecans; drizzle with butter. Bake for 40 minutes. Serve warm. Top with whipped cream.

Miss Daisy Entertains

The Peabody Hotel is a landmark in Memphis. The famous "Peabody Ducks" parade down to the lobby fountain twice daily to the delight of onlookers.

Old-Fashioned Molasses Stack Cake

This Molasses Stack Cake recipe is the one my mother used when I was a child. She always made one of these cakes for our Christmas breakfast. I still make one each Christmas, but I do not serve it for breakfast as she did. I dry my own apples each summer, for they are so much better than those bought in the supermarket.

⅔ cup shortening
⅔ cup sugar
⅔ cup molasses
2 eggs
6 cups all-purpose flour
1 teaspoon ginger

1 teaspoon cinnamon
3 teaspoons baking powder
2 teaspoons soda
¼ teaspoon salt
⅔ cup buttermilk

Cream together shortening, sugar and molasses. Add eggs, one at a time. Beat well after each egg is added. Sift flour, ginger, cinnamon, baking powder, soda and salt. Add dry ingredients and buttermilk alternatively to egg mixture. Divide batter into 5 or 6 parts. Pat into greased and floured 9-inch pans. Bake in a 400° oven until lightly browned. Spread each layer with dried apple filling. Do not put apples on top layer.

APPLE FILLING:
1 pound dried apples, cooked
    and mashed
1 cup brown sugar

1½ teaspoons cinnamon
½ teaspoon cloves
½ teaspoon allspice

Combine ingredients. Cool before spreading between cake layers.

The Original Tennessee Homecoming Cookbook

Yaourtopita II
Yogurt Nut Cake

1 cup soft butter	1 teaspoon cloves
1¼ cups sugar	1 cup yogurt
6 eggs, well beaten	2 teaspoons baking soda
2 cups flour	1 jigger whiskey
1 teaspoon cinnamon	1 cup finely chopped almonds

Beat butter and sugar together for 10 minutes. Add well beaten eggs, beat 5 minutes longer. Sift flour and spices together. Add to butter mixture gradually. Add yogurt, blend well. Dissolve baking soda in whiskey and add to mixture. Add almonds. Pour into greased 9 × 13-inch pan and bake 45 minutes at 350° or until toothpick comes out clean.

SYRUP:

2 cups sugar	1 stick cinnamon
3 cups water	

Combine syrup ingredients in saucepan, stir to dissolve sugar; bring to a boil; simmer (do not stir) for 10 minutes. When cake is completely cooled, cut into diamond or square shaped pieces and pour hot syrup over cake (while in pan) very slowly. Allow to set, undisturbed, at least 1 hour or until syrup is absorbed. Yield: 25–30 servings.

It's Greek to Me!

Cream Cheese Pound Cake

3 cups sugar
1½ cups butter or margarine
1 (8-ounce) package cream
   cheese
6 eggs

3 cups cake flour
1 teaspoon vanilla extract
1 teaspoon butter flavored
   extract

Cream sugar, butter and cream cheese together. Add eggs, one at a time, beating well after each addition. Stir in flavorings. Add flour and beat well. Pour into greased floured 10-inch tube or Bundt pan. Place in cold oven. Turn temperature on to 275° and bake for 1½ to 2 hours or until cake tests done. This is my favorite pound cake!

Tennessee's 95 Magic Mixes: Second Helping

Coconut Pound Cake

2 sticks butter or margarine
½ cup vegetable shortening
3 cups sugar
6 eggs
3 cups flour
1 cup milk

Dash of salt
½ teaspoon almond flavoring
½ teaspoon coconut flavoring
1 (3½-ounce) can grated
    coconut

Cream butter, shortening, and sugar. Add eggs, one at a time beating two minutes after each egg. Add flour and milk alternatively. Add salt and flavorings. Fold in coconut; pour into tube pan lined on bottom with waxed paper. Bake at 350° for 1 hour and 15 minutes. Start in COLD oven.

TOPPING:
1 cup sugar
1 cup water

1 teaspoon coconut flavoring

Boil 1 minute and pour over cake while hot. Serves 16–20.

The Nashville Cookbook

Pound Cake with Cherry Topping

Purchase pound cake. Place two slices on each dessert plate. Dip warm cherry topping over the cake at serving time.

CHERRY TOPPING:
8 ounces cherries (frozen, pitted,
    unsweetened)
2 tablespoons water
1 tablespoon cornstarch

2 tablespoons water
¼ cup sugar
1 tablespoon lemon juice

Place cherries and 2 tablespoons water into a small saucepan. Bring to boil; cook 1 minute.

In a cup combine the cornstarch, water, sugar, and lemon juice. Stir to dissolve the cornstarch and sugar in the liquid. Add to the warm cherries. Stir and cook on low heat to form a sauce (approximately 1–2 minutes). Serves 2.

More Home Cooking in a Hurry

The Apple Barn Fresh Apple Pound Cake
Luscious apple all the way and easy to make.

3 cups all-purpose flour,
  spooned into cup
1 teaspoon soda
1 teaspoon salt
1½ cups corn oil
2 cups sugar
3 large eggs, room temperature

2 teaspoons vanilla extract
1¼ cups pecans, medium-fine
  chopped
2 cups pared apples, finely
  chopped
Brown Sugar Topping

Sift flour, soda and salt onto a platter or waxed paper. In a large bowl beat oil, sugar, eggs and vanilla at medium speed of electric mixer for 3 or 4 minutes until well blended. Gradually add flour mixture; beat until smooth. Fold in pecans and apples. Pour batter into a greased and floured bundt pan. Bake in a preheated 325° oven about 1 hour 20 minutes, or until cake tests done. Cool on wire rack 20 minutes. For festive occasion, dribble brown sugar topping over warm cake. For an elegant dessert, slice cake and top each serving with baked custard. This cake is marvelous plain. Serve warm or cold. Store cake in foil or tin can for a day or two. To keep longer, refrigerate and bring to room temperature before serving. Fresh apples tend to mold easily. Yield: one 10-inch bundt cake, 22 to 24 servings.

BROWN SUGAR TOPPING:
½ cup butter or margarine
½ cup light brown sugar, firmly
  packed

2 teaspoons milk

Combine all ingredients and bring to a boil over medium heat; cook 2 minutes, stirring constantly. Spoon hot sugar mixture over warm cake.

The Apple Barn Cookbook

Tennessee Ernie Ford's Fresh Apple Nut Cake

2 eggs
1 cup oil
1¾ cups granulated sugar
2½ cups sifted self-rising flour
1 cup chopped nuts
3 cups pared, chopped apples
1 teaspoon cinnamon
1 teaspoon vanilla

Grease a 13×9×2-inch baking pan. Beat eggs, oil, and sugar together thoroughly. Add flour, nuts, apples, cinnamon, and vanilla; mix well. Turn the batter into the prepared pan and bake at 300° 1 hour 10 minutes. Yield: 8 to 10 servings.

CREAM CHEESE ICING:

2 (3-ounce) packages cream cheese
¼ cup butter or margarine, softened
1 (1-pound) box powdered sugar
2 teaspoons vanilla

Blend the icing ingredients until smooth. Frost the cooled cake. Store in the refrigerator.

Encore! Nashville

Cherry Topped Cheesecake

1 package yellow cake mix
4 eggs
2 tablespoons oil
2 packages, 8 ounces each, cream cheese, softened
½ cup sugar
1½ cups milk
3 tablespoons lemon juice
3 teaspoons vanilla
1 can cherry pie filling

Preheat oven to 300°. Reserve 1 cup of dry cake mix. In large mixing bowl, combine remaining cake mix, 1 egg and oil. Mixture will be crumbly. Press crust mixture evenly into bottom and ¾ of the way up the sides of a greased 13×9×2-inch pan or two 9-inch layer cake pans. In same bowl, blend cream cheese and sugar. Add 3 eggs and reserved cake mix. Beat 1 minute at medium speed. At low speed slowly add milk and flavorings; mix until smooth. Pour into crust. Bake at 300° for 35 to 45 minutes or if in 9-inch pans for 40 to 50 minutes until center is firm. When cool, top with pie filling; chill before serving. Store in refrigerator. Can also freeze covered with foil.

The Sevier County Cookbook

Almond Cheesecake

1 cup sugar
¼ cup butter
1 pound cream cheese
¼ cup cake flour (sifted before measuring)
2 tablespoons honey
5 eggs, separated (whites beaten stiff but not dry)

½ cup light cream
¼ teaspoon almond extract
1 teaspoon vanilla extract
½ cup finely chopped blanched almonds (measured after chopping)

TOPPING:
¼ cup light brown sugar
1 teaspoon cinnamon

¼ cup finely chopped almonds

Cream the butter and sugar together until well mixed. Add the cheese and enough cream until the mixture is fluffy. Blend in the flour and honey, then the egg yolks. Beat well after adding the egg yolks. Add remaining cream and extracts; then lightly fold in the beaten egg whites. Last fold in the chopped almonds with a few deft strokes, distributing them through the batter. Pour into a well-buttered spring form, sprinkle with topping mixture, set on low rack in 325° oven for 1 hour. Turn off heat and allow to cool in oven for 1 additional hour.

Grand Tour Collection

Cookies and Candies

Broadcast live from Opryland U.S.A. in Nashville every Friday and Saturday night, the Grand Ole Opry is the longest running radio show in the world.

$100 Brownies

1 stick butter	1 cup sifted all purpose flour
4 squares bitter chocolate	½ teaspoon salt
2 cups granulated sugar	1 teaspoons vanilla
4 eggs	

Melt over low heat in a heavy saucepan, 1 stick of real butter and 4 squares bitter chocolate. Let cool. Drop into the cooled mixture 2 cups of granulated sugar and stir until well mixed. Now add 4 eggs, one at a time, and mix well. Finally add 1 cup sifted all purpose flour, ½ teaspoon salt and 1 teaspoon vanilla.

Grease and flour a large cookie pan about 10 × 15 inches. Pour in the brownie batter and bake in a 350° oven for 20 to 25 minutes. You must watch to see that they don't overcook. Since they are thin, you must keep them on the soft and moist side. They are done when they first begin to pull away from the sides of the pan and get a dull look on the top.

$100 BROWNIE FROSTING:

½ stick butter	1½ teaspoons vanilla
1 square bitter chocolate	1½ teaspoons lemon juice
½ box powdered sugar	1 cup chopped pecans
1 egg	

Melt over low heat ½ stick butter and 1 square of bitter chocolate. When melted, add about ½ box of powdered sugar. Mix. Take off stove and add 1 egg. Mix well. Add 1½ teaspoons vanilla and 1½ teaspoons of lemon juice. This combination of flavors cuts the too-chocolate taste. Finally add 1 cup chopped pecans. Your consistency should be about right, but if not, add more powdered sugar. Remember that it is warm and will get harder. This acts as a chocolate pecan glaze, and should have a lovely sheen if it is put on while the brownies are warm. This frosting is the secret of the popularity of $100 Brownies.

Chattanooga Cook Book

Easy Brownies

18 graham cracker squares
1 can Eagle Brand milk
1 (6-ounce) package chocolate
  bits

Dash of salt

Roll graham crackers until fine, then mix with remaining ingredients. Pour into 8-inch square pan that has been greased and floured and bake 30 minutes in 350° oven. Cut in squares while still warm and remove from pan. Yield: 20–25 squares. (Nuts may be added, if desired.)

The Memphis Cookbook

Low-Sodium Brownies

½ cup unsalted margarine
6 tablespoons cocoa
¾ cup all-purpose plain flour

1 cup sugar
2 eggs, slightly beaten
1 teaspoon vanilla

Melt margarine and mix in the cocoa. Combine flour and sugar; add the margarine-cocoa mixture. Add eggs and vanilla. Stir until ingredients are combined. Pour into greased 9-inch square pan. Bake at 350° for 20–25 minutes. Cut into 16 squares. This makes a fudge-type brownie. Yield: 16 squares. Serving: 1 square; negligible sodium; 135 calories.

Tip: Unsalted nuts have negligible sodium content and may be added if desired.

Change of Seasons

Caramel Brownies

1 (14-ounce) package Kraft
  caramels
1 (5-ounce) can evaporated milk,
  divided
1 Pillsbury German Chocolate
  cake mix

1 stick butter
1 (6-ounce) package semi-sweet
  chocolate chips
1 cup pecans, optional

Melt caramels, ⅓ cup of the evaporated milk in double boiler; set aside. Mix cake mix, butter, and ⅓ cup evaporated milk until the consistency of dough. Add nuts. Take one half of the dough and press in the bottom of a greased 9 × 13 pan. Bake at 350° for 7 minutes. Sprinkle chips over baked mix. Pour melted caramels over chips. Put other half of the dough on top. Bake at 350° for 15 minutes. Cool and cut into squares.

Maury County Cookbook

Apple Brownies

⅔ cup soft margarine
1¾ cups brown sugar
2 eggs
1 teaspoon vanilla
2 cups flour
2 teaspoons baking powder

¼ teaspoon salt
1 cup chopped, peeled apples
⅓ cup chopped walnuts
⅓ cup raisins
Powdered sugar

Cream margarine and brown sugar. Add eggs and beat until well mixed. Add vanilla and mix again. Add sifted dry ingredients and beat until mixture is smooth. Add apples, walnuts and raisins and stir gently with a strong spoon. Spread batter in a greased 9 × 13-inch pan and bake at 350° for 30 to 35 minutes. Remove brownies from pan and roll each one in sifted powdered sugar. Yield: 1½ dozen.

The Apple Barn Cookbook

Low Calorie Peanut Butter Cookies

2½ cups sifted flour
½ teaspoon teaspoon baking
   soda
½ teaspoon baking powder
¼ teaspoon salt

6 tablespoons peanut butter
½ cup granulated sugar
   substitute
2 eggs

Preheat oven to 375°. Lightly grease cookie sheet. Sift together dry ingredients. Combine peanut butter and eggs. Add sugar substitute and mix well. Beat in dry ingredients. Drop by teaspoonsful onto cookie sheet. Flatten with fork in criss-cross pattern. Bake for 10 to 12 minutes. Yield: 32 cookies, 26 calories each.

Tennessee's 95 Magic Mixes: Second Helping

Chocolate Praline Cookies

⅔ cup butter
2 eggs
½ cup nuts, chopped
1½ cups flour
¼ teaspoon salt

2 cups brown sugar
1 teaspoon vanilla
2 cups chocolate chips
2 teaspoons baking powder

Melt butter and add to sugar, eggs and vanilla. Mix in the dry ingredients. Add nuts and chocolate chips. Bake in small rectangle pan. Bake 35 minutes in 350° oven. When cool, cut into bars.

Note: One and one-half this recipe makes a large rectangle pan of these cookies.

Parties & Pleasures

Chocolate Covered Cherry Cookies

1½ cups flour
½ cup cocoa
¼ teaspoon salt
¼ teaspoon baking powder
¼ teaspoon baking soda
½ cup butter or margarine
1 cup sugar
1 egg

1½ teaspoons vanilla
1 (10-ounce) jar maraschino
  cherries
1 (6-ounce) package semi-sweet
  chocolate morsels
½ cup sweetened condensed
  milk
4 teaspoons cherry juice

In a large bowl, stir together flour, cocoa, salt, baking powder, and baking soda; set aside. In mixing bowl, beat butter and sugar. Add egg and vanilla, mixing well; add dry ingredients. Shape dough into 1-inch balls. Place on ungreased cookie sheet. Press down center of dough with thumb and place a cherry in center. In small pan, combine chocolate chips and condensed milk and heat until chips are melted; stir in cherry juice. Spoon 1 teaspoon frosting over each cherry, spreading to cover cherry. Bake at 350° for 10 minutes. Yield: 48 cookies.

Flaunting Our Finest

Sugar Cookies

1 cup margarine	2 teaspoons vanilla
1 cup white sugar	4 cups flour
1 cup powdered sugar	1 teaspoon soda
2 eggs	½ teaspoon salt
1 cup oil	½ teaspoon cream of tartar

Cream together margarine, white and powdered sugars. Add eggs, oil and vanilla. Sift dry ingredients together and add to batter. Chill 2 hours. Make into balls the size of walnuts and place on ungreased cookie sheet. Flatten with bottom of glass dipped in sugar. Bake at 350° for about 8 minutes or until golden brown. You can add 1 teaspoon nutmeg, if desired.

Elvis Fans Cookbook

Yum-Yum Bars

½ cup butter	1 teaspoon baking powder
1 cup granulated sugar	1 egg white
1 egg and 1 egg yolk	1 cup light brown sugar, not
1 teaspoon vanilla	packed
1½ cups cake flour	1 cup pecans
½ teaspoon salt	

Mix first 7 ingredients and put in a greased 9 × 13 × 2-inch pan. Beat egg white until very stiff. Fold in brown sugar and pecans. Spread over batter and bake 25 to 30 minutes at 300°. Yield: 24 bars.

Note: These are a great favorite with both young and old.

Nashville Seasons

Three Layer Cookie

FIRST LAYER:

½ cup butter or margarine
1 square unsweetened chocolate
¼ cup sugar
1 teaspoon vanilla

1 egg, beaten
2 cups crushed graham crackers
½ cup chopped nuts
1 cup flaked coconut

Melt butter and chocolate in pan over low heat. Add sugar and vanilla and blend. Add beaten egg and cook for about 5 minutes or until egg is cooked. Add graham crackers, nuts and coconut. Press into 9 × 9-inch pan and chill for 15 minutes.

SECOND LAYER:

½ cup butter or margarine
2 tablespoons instant vanilla
  pudding mix

3 tablespoons milk
2 cups powdered sugar

Cream butter until fluffy. Add instant pudding mix, milk and powdered sugar. Beat until smooth and spread over first layer. Chill for 15 minutes.

THIRD LAYER:

4 squares semi-sweet chocolate   1 tablespoon butter

Melt chocolate squares with butter over low heat. Spread over second layer. Chill until firm and cut into small squares. These may be frozen.

Dixie Delights

Jack Daniels Distillery and George Dickel Distillery are the only places in the world where genuine Tennessee sour mash whiskey is produced.

Moonshine Cookies

½ pound crystallized cherries, chopped
½ pound crystallized pineapple, chopped

½ pound white raisins
¼ pound crystallized orange peel
¼ pound crystallized citron
1 cup good whiskey

Let fruits soak in whiskey overnight.
Now add:

1 pound nuts
3 cups flour
1 teaspoon ground cloves
1 teaspoon cinnamon

1 cup sugar
⅔ cup melted butter
3 eggs, beaten

Dissolve and add to above mixture:

1 teaspoon soda in
1 tablespoon buttermilk

Add vanilla to taste and drop by teaspoonfuls on greased cookie sheet. Bake in 325° oven 12–15 minutes. Keep in cookie jar until mellow. Great with boiled custard or vanilla ice cream.

Kountry Kooking

Chattanooga Chew Chews

CRUST:

2 cups all-purpose flour
1 cup brown sugar, firmly
  packed

½ cup butter (no substitute),
  softened
1 cup chopped pecans

Preheat oven to 350°. Mix flour, brown sugar and butter. Press into ungreased 9 × 13-inch pan. Sprinkle pecans evenly over unbaked crust.

CARAMEL TOPPING:

1 cup butter (no substitute)
¾ cup brown sugar

1 (12-ounce) package semi-sweet
  chocolate chips

For Caramel Topping melt butter and brown sugar in saucepan. Bring to a boil and boil for 1 minute, stirring constantly. Pour caramel mixture over crust and pecans. Bake for 20 to 25 minutes or until entire surface is bubbly. Remove from oven and sprinkle chocolate chips over hot surface. Gently swirl melted chocolate chips with spatula to give a marbled effect. Cool at least 5 hours. Cut into squares. Yield: 32 squares.

Dinner on the Diner

Raspberry Chocolate Sweets

1 cup butter, softened
1½ cups sugar, divided
2 egg yolks
2½ cups all-purpose flour
10 ounces raspberry jelly, jam or
  preserves

1 cup semi-sweet chocolate chips
4 egg whites
¼ teaspoon salt
2 cups chopped nuts

Preheat oven to 350°. Cream butter and ½ cup sugar. Add egg yolks; mix well. Add flour and blend. Spread on greased 10 × 15-inch jelly roll pan. Bake for 15 to 20 minutes.

Remove from oven, spread with jelly and sprinkle with chocolate chips. beat egg whites with salt until stiff. Gradually fold in remaining 1 cup sugar. Fold in nuts. Spread on top and bake an additional 25 minutes. Allow to cool before cutting. Yield: 4 dozen bars.

Dinner on the Diner

Praline Confection

20–24 graham crackers
1 cup butter or margarine
1 cup light brown sugar
  (packed)

1 cup chopped pecans

Line 15 × 10 × 1-inch jelly roll pan with whole graham crackers. Bring butter and sugar to rolling boil in medium saucepan. Boil for 2 minutes. Remove from heat. When bubbling has stopped, add nuts. Spoon over graham crackers. Bake at 350° for 10 minutes. Cut in squares. Keeps well in tightly covered container. Yield: 40 squares.

Dixie Delights

Omm Pah Pah Popcorn

16 cups popped popcorn, lightly
  salted
2 cups light brown sugar
½ cup white corn syrup

1 cup butter or margarine
½ teaspoon cream of tartar
1 teaspoon baking soda

Mix all ingredients except soda and popped corn together in sauce-pan. Dissolve over low heat, stirring constantly. Bring to boil and boil for 5 minutes on high. Remove from heat; add soda and pour over popped corn in large dishpan or bowl. Mix well and place in shallow baking pan in oven. Bake at 250° for 30 minutes stirring every few minutes. Store in tightly covered plastic or metal container.

Tennessee's 95 Magic Mixes: Second Helping

Chocolate Covered Cherries

4–5 jars of Maraschino cherries
  with stems
2 boxes powdered sugar
1 stick margarine, melted
1 can Eagle Brand milk

Pinch of salt
18 ounces Nestle's semi-sweet
  morsels
½ stick paraffin wax

Lay cherries on paper towels to drain well. Pat very dry. Mix powdered sugar, margarine, Eagle Brand, and salt; batter will be very stiff. Put in three separate bowls in freezer until very cold (not frozen). Take out one bowl at a time, working with mixture until it softens too much; then put bowl back in freezer and get a cold batch. Pinch off a small amount of batter; mash out into a thin sheet; wrap around cherry. As cherries are wrapped, stick in freezer until all are completed. Melt chocolate morsels and paraffin in double boiler or fondue pot. Dip cherries in chocolate, one at a time; let drain briefly in mid-air before placing on waxed paper to cool. Store cherries in freezer or refrigerator until an hour before serving.

Hints: Batter must be kept very cold at all times. Be sure confection wraps are thick enough to contain cherry juice; seal wrap well at stem. Paraffin is slow to melt; sliver before putting in pot with chocolate. This is a job that you'll need to reserve most of the day for, and invite a friend over to keep you company while you both work!

Koinonia Cooking

Peggy's Chocolate Bar Candy
This resembles a Heath Bar

1 pound butter
1 (16-ounce) box light brown
  sugar

½ pound chocolate bar
1 cup chopped pecans

In heavy saucepan, cook butter and brown sugar slowly to hard crack (300° on candy thermometer). Stir occasionally. While cooking, melt chocolate bar in double boiler. Grease $15 \times 10 \times 1$-inch jellyroll pan and sprinkle with pecans. Pour sugar mixture over chopped pecans. Spread melted chocolate over the pecans. Allow to cool and break into pieces.

Flaunting Our Finest

Divinity Fudge
This candy has a melt-in-your-mouth goodness.

2 cups sugar
½ cup white corn syrup
½ cup water
2 egg whites

$\frac{1}{16}$ teaspoon salt
1 tablespoon vanilla extract
½ cup broken pecans

Combine sugar, corn syrup, and water in saucepan. Place over medium heat and stir until dissolved. Boil without stirring, to hard ball stage when tested in cold water, or 265°. While syrup is cooking beat egg whites until stiff but not dry. Add salt and the hot syrup, pouring slowly at first, and then faster, beating constantly. When mixture is stiff, beat with a wooden spoon until creamy. Add nuts and extract. Pour into greased dish. Mark into 1-inch squares. Makes 24 squares.

Chopped candied cherries and pineapple may be added instead of nuts; almond extract may replace the vanilla.

The Nashville Cookbook

Rocky Road

1 (12-ounce) package (semi-sweet chocolate chips
1 (14-ounce) can sweetened condensed milk
2 tablespoons margarine

1 (10½-ounce) package (5½ cups) miniature marshmallows
1 (8-ounce jar) (1⅔ cups) unsalted roasted peanuts

In a saucepan, combine chocolate chips, sweetened condensed milk, and margarine. Heat over low heat till chocolate is melted; remove from heat. In a large bowl, combine marshmallows and peanuts. Fold in chocolate mixture. Spread in a 13×9×2-inch pan whose sides and bottom have been lined with wax paper. Chill 2 hours or till firm. Remove from pan, peel off wax paper and cut into 1-inch squares with a wet knife. Wrap pieces in plastic wrap. Makes 8 dozen.

The Sevier County Cookbook

Coconut Bonbons

1 can Eagle Brand milk
½ stick margarine
2 cups pecans, chopped
1 teaspoon vanilla
1 stick margarine

2 boxes powdered sugar
2 cans Angel flake coconut
1 block parafin
2 packages chocolate chips

Mix milk, ½ stick margarine, pecans, powdered sugar, coconut and vanilla and form into walnut-sized balls. In double boiler, melt together parafin, one stick margarine, and chocolate chips. Dip each ball until coated, using round toothpick. Put on dish to dry.

Joyce's Favorite Recipes

Pies and Desserts

Skiing at Gatlinburg, Gateway to the Smokies.

Bourbon and Chocolate Pecan Pie

This pie is labeled *Jackson Pie* on Miss Daisy's Menu. Pierre Franey, food critic for the *New York Times,* described this as one of the best pecan pies he had eaten, while at a luncheon I served that he attended.

1 cup sugar	2 tablespoons bourbon
¼ cup butter, melted	1 teaspoon vanilla
3 eggs, slightly beaten	½ cup pecans, chopped
¾ cup light corn syrup	½ cup chocolate chips
¼ teaspoon salt	1 (9-inch) pie shell

Cream sugar and butter. Add eggs, syrup, salt, bourbon and vanilla. Mix until blended. Spread pecans and chocolate chips in bottom of pie shell. Pour filling into shell. Bake in a 375° oven for 40 to 50 minutes. Yield: 6 to 8 servings.

The Original Tennessee Homecoming Cookbook

Lemon Chess Pie

4 eggs	¼ cup melted butter
1½ cups sugar	¼ cup lemon juice
1 tablespoon cornmeal	1 tablespoon grated lemon rind
1 tablespoon all-purpose flour	1 unbaked (9-inch) pie shell
¼ cup cream	

Beat eggs until creamy. Thoroughly mix sugar, meal, and flour. Add to eggs. Slowly add cream, butter, lemon juice, and rind; mix well. Pour into pie shell and bake 40–50 minutes at 350°. Makes one 9-inch pie.

The James K. Polk Cookbook

Pecan Pie

1½ cups brown sugar	1 teaspoon vanilla
2 tablespoons cornmeal	½ stick margarine
2 tablespoons cold water	½ cup chopped pecans
2 whole eggs, well beaten	1 unbaked pie shell

Combine all ingredients. Mix well. Pour into pie shell. Bake 15 minutes at 375° and turn oven to 350°. Bake 30 minutes longer or until firm. (Could be less than 30 minutes.)

This recipe was given to me by my mother-in-law in 1945. This recipe is the most prized recipe in the Thomas family. (Three generations)

Family Favorites by the Miller's Daughters

Pumpkin Pie

¾ cup brown sugar	1½ cups canned pumpkin
1 tablespoon all-purpose flour	1⅓ cups evaporated milk
½ teaspoon salt	1 egg, slightly beaten
2¼ teaspoons pumpkin pie spices	1 (8-inch) unbaked pastry shell

Preheat over to 375°. Combine brown sugar, flour, salt, and spices. Stir in pumpkin, milk, and egg. Mix until smooth. Pour into unbaked pastry shell.

Bake for about 45 minutes. Remove from oven and spread Nut Topping around edge. Bake 15 minutes more. Serve warm or cold.

NUT TOPPING:

½ cup chopped pecans	1 tablespoon butter or
1½ teaspoons grated orange rind	margarine
	2 tablespoons brown sugar

Combine all ingredients. Use as directed. Makes 6 servings.

Minnie Pearl Cooks

Grasshopper Pie and Chocolate Wafer Crust

24 marshmallows
½ cup milk
¼ cup creme de menthe

1 cup heavy cream
1 (9-inch) chocolate wafer crust

Melt marshmellows in milk. Let cool. Add creme de menthe. Whip cream and fold into mixture.

CRUST:

¾ cup chocolate cookie crumbs 3 ounces butter, melted

Combine crumbs and butter and press into a 9-inch pan.

Recipes from Miss Daisy's

French Silk Chocolate Pie

MERINGUE PIE CRUST:

2 egg whites
⅛ teaspoon salt
⅛ teaspoon cream of tartar

½ cup sugar
½ cup chopped pecans
1 teaspoon vanilla

Beat egg whites, salt and cream of tartar until foamy. Add sugar gradually and beat until stiff. Fold in pecans and vanilla. Place in greased 9-inch pie plate, building up sides ½ inch. Bake 1 hour at 300°. Cool.

FILLING:

1 stick butter, softened
¾ cup sugar
2 squares unsweetened
  chocolate, melted

1½ teaspoons vanilla
2 egg yolks
2 whole eggs
1 cup heavy cream, whipped

Cream butter and sugar. Blend in chocolate and vanilla. Add eggs and yolks, one at a time, beating 5 minutes between each one. Do not underbeat! Pour into cooled crust and refrigerate. Decorate with whipped cream and shaved chocolate if desired. Serves 8.

Well Seasoned

Black Bottom Pie

CRUST:

1⅓ cups crushed gingersnaps
⅓ cup soft butter

2 tablespoons sugar
1 bar German chocolate, divided

Mix gingersnaps, butter and sugar. Shave chocolate, and add one-half to gingersnap mixture, stirring well. Press into bottom and sides of 9-inch pie pan; bake in 350° oven 10 minutes.

FILLING:

1 package vanilla pudding mix
2 cups light cream
⅓ cup white rum
1 package chocolate pudding
   mix

1½ cups milk
½ cup heavy cream, whipped

Blend together vanilla pudding mix, 1½ cups light cream and rum. Bring to a boil, stirring constantly. Pour into pie crust, cover with waxed paper, chill. Blend together chocolate pudding mix, ½ cup light cream, milk and remaining half of shaved chocolate. Bring to a boil, stirring constantly. Pour over first layer. Cover with waxed paper and chill. Before serving remove waxed paper and top with whipped cream.

Woman's Exchange Cookbook II

Strawberry Almond Pie

1 (3-ounce) package strawberry
  Jello
1 (3-ounce) package vanilla
  pudding, regular
1¼ cups water

1½ pints strawberries, sliced
½ cup toasted, chopped almonds
¼ teaspoon almond flavoring
Cool Whip to garnish

Combine Jello, vanilla pudding and water. Bring to a boil. Remove from heat and stir in the sliced strawberries and flavoring (also almonds, if desired). Let stand 5 minutes, then pour in baked pie shell. Chill until set (3 or 4 hours). Garnish with Cool Whip and sprinkle nuts on top, if they were not added to filling, or use both ways.

Gatlinburg Recipe Collection

Delicate Raspberry Pie

My aunt who said she couldn't cook gave me this great recipe.

1 envelope unflavored gelatin
¼ cup orange juice
½ cup sugar

2 cups mashed raspberries
1 cup cream, whipped
1 graham cracker crust

Sprinkle gelatin over orange juice and heat until dissolved. Add sugar to berries (check for personal taste); combine with gelatin mixture. Fold in whipped cream and pour into crust. Swirl top with fork. Chill for 24 hours before serving.

. . . and garnish with Memories

Chattanooga was the site of one of the bloodiest battles of the Civil War. The Chickamauga-Chattanooga Battlefield is the nation's oldest, largest, and most visited national military park.

Mother's Suiter's Fresh Peach Pie

CRUST:

3 tablespoons light brown sugar   1 stick margarine
1 cup flour

Combine brown sugar and flour; cut in margarine. Press into a
12 × 8-inch baking dish. Bake at 325° for 8 to 10 minutes.

FILLING:

3 fresh peaches
¼ cup sugar

Peel and thinly slice peaches. Add ¼ cup sugar and let stand for 1
hour.

1 cup sugar   2 tablespoons margarine
6 tablespoons flour   1 cup whipping cream
¼ teaspoon salt   ¼ cup sugar
1 cup water

Mix sugar, flour and salt together thoroughly. Add water and cook
over medium heat until thick. Add margarine and cool, then add
peaches. Whip cream with sugar and fold into peach mixture. Pour
into prepared crust and refrigerate. Yield: 8 servings.

Out of this World

Quick Strawberry Cream Pie

1 package strawberry gelatin   1 tablespoon lemon juice
1 cup boiling water   1 cup whipping cream, whipped
1 package frozen strawberries,   2 egg whites, beaten (optional)
  thawed   Baked pastry shell

Dissolve the gelatin in the boiling water. Add the frozen strawberries, juice and all, and the lemon juice. Let cool. Fold in the
whipped cream, pour in a baked shell and chill. Or fold in the
whites, beaten stiff, along with the whipped cream and chill.

Chattanooga Cook Book

Crisp Crust Apple Pie

FILLING:

5 medium apples (Red or
   Golden Delicious)
1½ cups sugar
1 tablespoon flour

1 teaspoon cinnamon (more or
   less depending on taste)
½ cup water

Slice apples thin into an oblong baking dish. Mix together sugar, flour and cinnamon, sprinkle over apples. Pour water over mixture.

CRUST:

2½ cups self-rising flour
½ teaspoon salt
⅔ cup shortening
About ½ cup ice water

¾ cup sugar
1 teaspoon cinnamon
½ cup butter or margarine

Mix flour and salt; cut in shortening. Add enough water to hold dough together. Roll between sheets of waxed paper. Put on top of apple mixture. Sprinkle on sugar and cinnamon (mixed together). Dot with butter cut into patties. Bake at 400° until crust is browned and apples are tender. (When I have been in a rush, I have used 2 frozen pie shells for crust and put on topping).

The Apple Barn Cookbook

Cracker Pie

3 egg whites
1 cup sugar
¼ teaspoon baking powder
Pinch salt

20 chopped dates
½ cup nuts chopped
12 soda crackers, rolled fine

Beat egg whites until stiff. Add sugar, baking powder and salt gradually. Mix in other ingredients. Pour in greased pie pan and cook in 350° oven for 20 minutes. Do not over bake. Wonderful hot or cold. Whipped cream or ice cream topping can be used, but is good plain.

Cracker Barrel Old Country Stores:
Old Timey Recipes & Proverbs to Live By

Graham Apple Pie
A distinctive flavor

1 cup sugar	1 tablespoon cornstarch
½ cup water	⅓ cup water
½ stick butter	1½ teaspoons brandy extract
4 or 5 apples, sliced thin	1 unbaked pie shell
1 tablespoon lemon juice	

To boiling sugar-water-butter, add sliced apples, return to boil. Lift apples and place in pie shell.

Combine lemon juice, cornstarch and one-third cup water. Add to sugar mixture. Cook until thickened. Remove from heat, add brandy flavoring. Pour over apples.

Add topping and bake at 400° for about 35 minutes.

TOPPING:

½ cup graham cracker crumbs	Dash cinnamon
1 tablespoon flour	Dash nutmeg
2 tablespoons sugar	1 tablespoon butter

Mix dry ingredients and blend in the butter. Spread on pie.

Sam Houston Schoolhouse Cookbook

Apple Dumplings

2 cups all-purpose flour
2 teaspoons baking powder
1 teaspoon salt
1 tablespoon butter or
  margarine, softened
1 tablespoon shortening
1 cup milk

½ cup butter or margarine,
  melted
1 teaspoon ground cinnamon
4 tablespoons brown sugar
6 tart apples, peeled, cored and
  chopped
Apple Dumpling Sauce

Combine flour, baking powder and salt in a large mixing bowl. Cut in butter and shortening until mixture resembles coarse meal. Gradually add milk to make a soft dough. Roll dough into a ¼-inch thick rectangle on a lightly floured surface. Brush with melted butter; sprinkle with cinnamon and brown sugar. Spread apples over pastry. Roll up jellyroll fashion; cut into 10 slices. Place flat in a greased 13 × 9 × 2-inch baking pan; bake at 350° for 20 minutes. Pour Apple Dumpling Sauce over top, and continue baking 20 minutes. Yield: 10 servings.

APPLE DUMPLING SAUCE:

1 cup sugar
1 tablespoon all-purpose flour
Dash of salt

1 tablespoon butter or
  margarine
½ teaspoon lemon juice
1 cup hot water

Combine all ingredients in a saucepan over medium heat. Bring to a boil; cook 2 minutes, stirring constantly. Yield: 1½ cups.

The Apple Barn Cookbook

Shoo Fly Pie

3 cups flour
1 cup brown sugar
¾ cup butter
1 cup molasses

1 cup hot water
1 teaspoon baking soda
Few drops vinegar
2 unbaked pie crusts

Blend flour, sugar and butter until lumpy and save for topping. Blend molasses, hot water, soda and vinegar. Pour mixture into pie crusts, not baked. Top with crumb mixture and bake in a 350° oven for 35 minutes. This makes 2 pies.

Cracker Barrel Old Country Stores:
Old Timey Recipes & Proverbs to Live By

Perfect Custard Pie

Daddy's favorite pie, this is the recipe I used when I was doing a cooking program on WJHL-TV in the 1950's. I cut the pie while it was still warm and custard pie spilled across Channel 11's viewing area that day! But it is an excellent recipe if you chill it before serving.

1 (9-inch) unbaked pie shell
4 eggs, slightly beaten
½ cup sugar
¼ teaspoon salt

½ teaspoon vanilla
½ teaspoon almond
2½ cups scalded milk
Nutmeg

Let pie shell chill while you make the filling. Blend eggs, sugar, salt, vanilla and almond. Stir in *scalded milk—that is the secret to this pie.* Put your prepared crust into oven, which has been preheated to 400°, and let it bake for about 5 minutes. Leave pie pan on oven rack, pour filling into the pastry, then gently move rack into oven. Bake pie at 400° for 25 to 30 minutes. Test for doneness by inserting a silver knife into center of pie; if it comes out clean, the pie is done. Sprinkle top generously with nutmeg. Set pie on cooling rack for 30 minutes. Chill thoroughly in refrigerator before serving.

To scald milk: Heat until milk reaches boiling point, but do not let it boil. When tiny bubbles form around edge of pan, remove from heat. To scald milk in microwave, use temperature probe and heat to 180°.

. . . and garnish with Memories

Cheese Pie
(Kase Kuchen)

1 cup sugar
1 heaping teaspoon flour or
  bread crumbs
3 eggs

2 cups cottage cheese
Grated rind and juice of 1 lemon
1 baked pastry shell
6 tablespoons powdered sugar

Mix sugar and flour, reserving 2 egg whites; beat remaining egg white and yolks, then add with cottage cheese and lemon rind and juice in double cooker. Cook until thick.

This can be turned into the uncooked pastry shell and baked in a 350° oven for 40 minutes. The reserved whites of the egg may be beaten with 6 tablespoons,powdered sugar. Return to 325° oven and bake for seven more minutes.

Das Germantown Kochbuch

Heavenly Pie

1½ cups sugar
¼ teaspoon cream of tartar
4 eggs, separated
3 tablespoons lemon juice

1 tablespoon lemon rind, grated
⅛ teaspoon salt
1 pint heavy cream, whipped

Beat egg whites until stiff but not dry. Sift together 1 cup sugar and cream of tartar. Gradually add dry ingredients to beaten egg whites; continue to beat until thoroughly blended. Use this meringue to line bottom and sides of well-greased 9- or 10-inch pie pan, hollowing out most of center and being careful not to spread too close to the rim. Bake at 275° for one hour. Let cool.

Beat egg yolks slightly; stir in remaining sugar, lemon juice, rind and salt. Cook over boiling water until very thick, about 10 minutes. Allow to cool. Whip cream and combine half of it with the lemon-egg mixture. Fill meringue shell. Cover with remaining whipped cream. Chill overnight or about 24 hours.

Gatlinburg Recipe Collection

Amaretto Cheese Pie

CRUST:

1½ cups chocolate wafers, crushed into fine crumbs
1 cup blanched almonds, crushed into fine pieces
⅓ cup sugar
1 stick butter, melted

Make a crust by mixing the chocolate wafers, almonds, sugar, and butter. Press into two greased Pyrex pie pans.

FILLING:

1 (8-ounce) package soft cream cheese
1 cup sugar
3 egg yolks
1 tablespoon Amaretto liqueur
½ pint whipping cream
3 egg whites
1 small package blanched almonds, sliced

In a mixing bowl, cream the cream cheese with sugar. Beat until fluffy. Add egg yolks and Amaretto. In a separate bowl, whip the whipping cream until stiff and fold into the cheese mixture. In a separate bowl, beat the egg whites until stiff and fold into the cheese mixture. Pour into the chocolate crust. Freeze. When ready to serve, sprinkle the top of the pie with sliced almonds browned in butter. Pour one tablespoon Amaretto over each slice. This pie is so good it almost takes your breath away!

Gazebo Gala

Apricot Whip

This is a delicious, nutritious dessert—worth the few extra minutes it takes to prepare it.

1 cup whipping cream
1 (7¾-ounce) jar junior food,
 apricots with tapioca

1–2 tablespoons sugar

Whip cream; fold in apricots and sugar. Turn into sherbet glasses. Keep refrigerated until serving time.

Home Cooking in a Hurry

Tavola Pie

3 sticks sweet butter
¼ cup chopped walnuts
1 cup coarsely crushed vanilla
 wafers
1 cup confectioners' sugar
1 bottle imitation brandy extract

3 eggs
Apricot preserves
8 tablespoons regular brandy
1 pint heavy whipping cream
4 tablespoons confectioners'
 sugar

CRUST: Butter 9-inch Pyrex pie pan. Melt 1 stick butter. Combine walnuts, vanilla wafers, and butter (may not take all of butter). Press into pie pan. Do not make crust too thin or crush wafers and nuts too fine. Bake for about 8 minutes or until golden.

FILLING: Combine 2 sticks softened butter with 1 cup confectioners' sugar; whip well. Add ½ bottle brandy extract; whip. Add 3 whole eggs; whip well again. Spread on cooled pie crust. Refrigerate until firm. When firm, spread layer of apricot preserves to which you have added 4 tablespoons brandy.

TOPPING: Combine 1 pint whipping cream, 4 tablespoons confectioners' sugar, ½ bottle brandy extract, and 4 tablespoons brandy. Whip until firm; spread on pie. Refrigerate to chill.

Very rich and better if made the day before serving. This recipe came from a small Italian restaurant in New York City. It is one of the three desserts they serve.

Gazebo Gala

Bourbon Peaches
Just enough zing

1 (16-ounce) can peach halves
6 macaroons, crumbled
4 tablespoons butter or
   margarine, melted
1 (1¾-ounce) package pecan
   halves

1 tablespoon brown sugar
2 tablespoons bourbon
Salt

Place peach halves in muffin tins to help keep their shape. Fill cavities with a mixture of the remaining ingredients and bake in 300° oven for 15 minutes. Yield: 6 servings.

Encore! Nashville

Cherry Trifle

An elegance with ease dessert. Prepare and serve it in a glass bowl, so everyone can enjoy its beauty. If you wish, make it hours before serving.

1 package ladyfingers
Jelly (your favorite)
1 (5⅝-ounce) package vanilla
   pudding mix (not instant)

1 (16-ounce) can pitted dark
   sweet cherries, drained
Whipped cream if desired

Split ladyfingers; spread tops and bottoms with jelly. Sandwich ladyfingers back together. Place ladyfingers in bottom of bowl and around sides of the bowl. (Stand them up like children holding hands and walking around.)

Cook pudding mixture, following package directions. Pour some of the pudding over ladyfingers in bottom of the bowl. Arrange a layer of fruit on top of the pudding. Repeat layers again. Top with fruit and whipped cream. Store in refrigerator until serving time.

Home Cooking in a Hurry

Black Forest Cherries Flambe
(Schwarzwalder Kirschen Flambiert)

1 can (16-ounce) dark sweet
   cherries
2 teaspoons cornstarch
¼ cup Kirsch

½ cup Cherry flavored brandy
1 quart vanilla ice cream

Pour cherry juice into chafing dish and bring to a boil. Mix cornstarch with Kirsch until smooth, add to juice and cook slowly, stirring constantly until thickened and clear. Add cherries and cook 2 minutes longer. Pour brandy over cherries; ignite. Ladle while flaming over individual servings of vanilla ice cream. Serves 6–8.

Das Germantown Kochbuch

Roan Mountain, one of the tallest peaks in the eastern United States, is famous for its magnificent display of rhododendrons. In late June, the 600-acre garden paints the mountaintop with spectacular pink and purple blossoms.

Cherry Gelatin Jubilee

1 (6-ounce) package cherry or
  raspberry gelatin
1 (20-ounce) can crushed
  pineapple, drained
2 bananas, sliced
1 cup packed shredded coconut
  (no sodium added; check
  label)

½ cup unsalted nuts, chopped
3 cups whipped topping
1 (8-ounce) package cream
  cheese
1 (21-ounce) can cherry pie
  filling

In a 3-quart serving bowl, prepare gelatin according to package directions. Chill until slightly congealed. Fold in pineapple, bananas, coconut, nuts, and 2 cups whipped topping. Refrigerate until firm. Allow cream cheese to soften and whip until creamy. Fold in remaining 1 cup whipped topping. Spread over the top of the gelatin and refrigerate again until the cheese becomes more firm. Top with a layer of cherry pie filling.

This is delicious as a salad or dessert.

Tip: Other low-sodium fruits such as strawberries, peaches, or canned fruit may be substituted for the pineapple and bananas. Try other gelatin flavors.

Change of Seasons

Amaretto Cream Mold

1 envelope unflavored gelatin	Salt to taste
¼ cup cold water	½ cup Arametto liqueur
3 eggs, separated	1 cup whipping cream, whipped
½ cup sugar, divided	Slivered almonds, optional

Sprinkle gelatin over water in cup. In medium saucepan, beat egg yolks, ¼ cup sugar and salt. Add gelatin and water. Mix well. Place over medium heat and stir until gelatin and sugar are dissolved and mixture coats a spoon, about 5 minutes. Remove from heat and add Amaretto. Cool, stirring occasionally, until mixture gels slightly. Beat egg whites until they form soft peaks; add ¼ cup sugar gradually while beating until stiff. Fold egg whites into gelatin mixture; then fold whipped cream into mixture. Pour into serving bowl and chill in refrigerator. Garnish with slivered almonds, if desired. Serves 8.

Maury County Cookbook

Charlotte Russe

Charlotte Russe is reported to have been a favorite dessert of Captain Thomas Green Ryman, for whom The Ryman Auditorium was named. The sweet delicacy appeared on many early Nashville menus.

1½ tablespoons unflavored gelatin	1½ cups milk, scalded
½ cup cold water	⅛ teaspoon salt
2 egg yolks	2 egg whites, beaten
¾ cup sugar	1 cup cream, whipped
	1 teaspoon vanilla

Soak gelatin in cold water for 5 minutes. Beat egg yolks, sugar, and milk together and cook in double boiler; dissolve softened gelatin and salt in the hot mixture. When thick, remove from heat and cool. Fold in beaten egg whites, whipped cream, and vanilla. Pour into a 1-quart mold. Chill and serve.

The Nashville Cookbook

Betty's Pistachio Dessert

½ cup nuts, chopped fine
1 cup plain flour
1 stick butter, melted
1 (8-ounce) package cream
  cheese, softened

3 cups milk
1 cup confectioners sugar
1 (9-ounce) carton Cool Whip
2 small packages pistachio
  pudding (instant)

Stir together nuts, flour, butter and press in the bottom of a greased 9×13-inch Pyrex dish. Bake at 350° for 15–20 minutes. Cool completely. Mix cream cheese and confectioners' sugar until smooth. Fold in half of Cool Whip. Spread over cooled crust. Mix pudding and milk with electric mixer for 2 minutes. Spread over cheese mixture. Frost with remaining Cool Whip. Chill.

Cookin' & Quiltin'

¼c plus 2 T sugar. C flour + butter

More than any other state in the nation, Tennessee borders eight states: Kentucky, Virginia, North Carolina, Georgia, Alabama, Mississippi, Arkansas, and Missouri.

Pots de Creme

1 (6-ounce) package semisweet
  chocolate pieces
2 tablespoons sugar
Pinch of salt
1 egg

1 teaspoon vanilla
1½ teaspoons dark rum
¾ cup scalded milk
Whipped cream

Place first 6 ingredients in blender. Heat milk to boiling; pour into blender over other ingredients. Cover and blend one minute. Pour into demitasse cups or sherbet glasses. Chill several hours. Top with whipped cream. Yield: 4 servings.

Miss Daisy Entertains

Peaches Amaretto

6 tablespoons butter (do not use margarine)
1 peach per person, peeled and sliced
¼ teaspoon nutmeg
Sugar to taste

1 tablespoon vanilla
Juices of 1 lemon, 1 orange
1 teaspoon orange zest
1 teaspoon lemon zest
¼–½ cup Amaretto

In a heavy skillet, melt butter and add peaches. Sprinkle with nutmeg and sugar. Sauté until a bit syrupy. Add vanilla, juices and zests. Stir occasionally. Add Amaretto, warmed and ignited. Stir well and serve over vanilla ice cream, in a crepe, or topped with whipped cream. Yield: 6 to 8 servings.

Out of this World

Bananas au Rhum

6 bananas
1 cup fresh orange juice
2 tablespoons lemon juice

½ cup brown sugar
¼ cup Jamaican rum
Melted butter

Butter large baking dish. Peel and slice bananas lengthwise, then across in half. Lay bananas in dish, cut side up. Mix juices and rum together. Sprinkle brown sugar over bananas, carefully pour juice mixture over bananas plus a little melted butter. Bake in 400° oven 15 to 20 minutes. Baste with juice several times. Serves 6.

Equally good with meat or served cold with vanilla ice cream for dessert.

Woman's Exchange Cookbook II

Nutty Peach Crisp

1 (29-ounce) can sliced peaches with syrup (or frozen peaches)	½ cup butter, melted
1 package Betty Crocker butter pecan cake mix	1 cup flaked coconut
	1 cup chopped pecans

Heat oven to 325°. Layer ingredients in order listed in $13 \times 9 \times 2$-inch ungreased oblong pan, about 45 minutes.

Family Favorites by the Miller's Daughters

Q.E.D.
Quick–Easy–Delicious!

1 (16-ounce) can sliced peaches
1 (17-ounce) can unpeeled
  apricot halves
1 lemon, sliced
1⅓ cups prepared biscuit mix
2 tablespoon sugar

⅓ cup plus 1 tablespoon water
⅓ cup melted butter or
  margarine
1 (3-ounce) package slivered
  almonds

Heat oven to 450 °. Place peaches, apricots, and sliced lemon in a 1½-quart casserole. Bake for 20 minutes. Combine biscuit mix, sugar, and water. Remove the casserole from oven and drop the biscuit mixture in 6 or 8 portions on the bubbling fruit. Place casserole back in the oven and bake for 7 or 8 minutes. Melt the butter until hot, but not browned, then add silvered almonds. Sprinkle the buttered almonds on the casserole and continue baking until browned. Sprinkle lightly with salt. Serves 6–8.

The Nashville Cookbook

Chocolate Fried Pies

2 tablespoons cocoa
½ cup sugar

1 stick butter
Favorite pie dough recipe

Mix together sugar and cocoa. Roll out pie dough very thinly and cut in saucer size rounds. Place 1 tablespoon of sugar and cocoa mixture in center of pie round; top cocoa mixture with pat of butter. Fold and crimp edges together with a fork. Fry one side at a time until golden brown.

Cookin' & Quiltin'

Mocha Meringue

4 egg whites
⅔ cup sugar
1 cup chopped pecans
¼ cup light corn syrup
1 tablespoon instant coffee
1 (6-ounce) package semi-sweet
   chocolate chips

⅔ cup condensed milk
1½ cups heavy cream, divided
1 teaspoon vanilla
Shaved chocolate

Beat egg whites until soft peaks form. Add sugar, beating until stiff peaks form. Fold in pecans. Mold around sides and bottom of a greased and floured 9-inch pie plate, forming a high edge. Bake at 275° for 1 hour. Turn off oven. Cool in oven 2 hours. Mix syrup, coffee and 1 tablespoon water in saucepan. Bring to a boil. Reduce heat and add chocolate. Stir until melted. Remove from heat and stir in milk, 1 cup of cream and vanilla. Cover and chill 1 hour. Whip mixture until soft peaks form. Fill meringue shell with mixture and freeze overnight. Whip remaining ½ cup cream. Spread over dessert. Decorate with shaved chocolate, if desired. Serves 8.

Well Seasoned

Chocolate Mousse

My son Kerwin's very favorite dessert.

⅓ cup hot coffee
1 (6-ounce) package chocolate
   chips
4 eggs, separated

2 tablespoons creme de cacao
Whipped cream
Sliced toasted almonds

Combine coffee and chocolate chips in blender; process until smooth. Add egg yolks and creme de cacao; process 1 minute. Beat egg whites until stiff; fold chocolate mixture into egg whites. Spoon into individual serving dishes. Chill until set. Top with whipped cream and almonds.

. . .and garnish with Memories

Grand Marnier Soufflé

3 tablespoons butter
2 tablespoons flour
⅔ cup milk
½ cup sugar
¼ teaspoon salt

1 teaspoon vanilla
½ cup Grand Marnier
5 eggs, separated
6–8 lady fingers
Vanilla ice cream

Melt butter in saucepan; blend well with flour, gradually add milk, stirring constantly. Add sugar, salt and vanilla. When sauce is thick and smooth, remove from fire and cool. Add Grand Marnier, beaten yolks, stir; fold in stiffly beaten egg whites. Butter 2-quart Pyrex baking dish, sprinkle with sugar; crumble lady fingers sprinkled to taste with additional Grand Marnier; cover with batter. Cook in 400° oven for 15 minutes; cut heat to 375° for 15 more minutes. In blender whip vanilla ice cream, lightly flavored with additional Grand Marnier. Serve over souffle. Serves 4–6.

Woman's Exchange Cookbook I

Hot Fruit Bisque

12 macaroons, crumbled
4 cups peaches or any other fruit
½ cup almonds, slivered and
  toasted

¼ cup brown sugar
½ cup sherry
¼ cup melted butter

Butter 2½-quart casserole. Cover bottom with macaroon crumbs, alternate fruit and macaroons in layers, finishing with macaroons. Sprinkle with almonds, sugar, sherry, and melted butter. Bake in 350° oven for 30 minutes. Serve hot. Serves 8 to 10.

Woman's Exchange Cookbook I

The Colonel's Boiled Custard

6 eggs
3 cups sugar
½ gallon milk
2 tablespoons cornstarch

½ package miniature
  marshmallows
2 teaspoons vanilla

Beat the 6 eggs, then add sugar. In double boiler, heat ½ quart of the milk until it comes just to the boiling point. Take 2 cups of hot milk and mix well with the cornstarch. Slowly add this to egg and sugar mixture, stirring constantly. Then add the egg mixture to the rest of the milk. Stir custard slowly over medium heat, in double boiler, until custard thickens. Add ½ package of marshmallows and stir until marshmallows are dissolved. Remove from heat and let cool. Add 2 teaspoons vanilla and chill immediately. Serves 8 to 12.

A Man's Taste

Bread and Butter Pudding
This is my favorite

1⅓ cups sugar
¾ cup butter
8 slices bread
2 cups powdered sugar

5 cups milk
4 eggs
1 teaspoon nutmeg

Cream together sugar and butter; spread on trimmed bread slices. Cut each slice into 4 squares. Place in greased baking dish. Mix remaining ingredients and pour over bread. Bake in 350° oven for 30 minutes. Serve warm with a dab of whipped cream.

Kountry Kooking

Frosty Strawberry Squares

1 cup sifted flour	1 cup sugar
¼ cup brown sugar	2 cups sliced fresh strawberries
½ cup chopped walnuts or	or 10-ounce package frozen,
pecans	partially thawed
½ cup butter, melted	2 teaspoons lemon juice
2 egg whites	1 cup heavy cream, whipped

Stir together first four ingredients, spread evenly in shallow baking pan. Bake 20 minutes in 350° oven, stirring occasionally. Sprinkle ⅔ of this crumbed mixture in a 13 × 9 × 2-inch baking pan. Combine egg whites, sugar, berries and lemon juice in a large bowl. Beat at high speed until stiff peaks form about 10 minutes. Fold in whipped cream. Top with remaining crumbed mixture. Freeze 6 hours or overnight. Cut in squares. Top with fresh strawberries. Yield: 15 squares, 2½ × 3 inches.

Woman's Exchange Cookbook I

Frozen Crème de Menthe Pie

2 cups crushed chocolate wafers	6 tablespoons light cream
5½ tablespoons butter, softened	½ cup sugar
½ gallon vanilla ice cream	Dash of salt
7 tablespoons green crème de	3 tablespoons butter
menthe	1 teaspoon vanilla
2 (1-ounce) squares	
unsweetened chocolate	

Combine wafer crumbs with softened butter. Press into a 9-inch springform pan. Refrigerate at least one hour. Turn ice cream into large bowl to soften. Stir crème de menthe into ice cream. Fill wafer shell with ice cream mixture and freeze. Melt chocolate squares in cream over low heat. Add sugar and salt. Remove from heat and add butter and vanilla. Stir until cooled. Let stand until cooled thoroughly. When pie is frozen, spread chocolate sauce over top. Return to freezer until firm. Serves 10.

Delicious and easy. Men love it.

Well Seasoned

Frozen Soufflé with Hot Strawberry Sauce

½ gallon vanilla ice cream
12 almond macaroons, crumbled
5 tablespoons Grand Marnier

2 cups heavy cream
½ cup chopped toasted almonds
Powdered sugar

Soften ice cream slightly. Stir in crumbled macaroons and Grand Mariner. Whip cream until thick and shiny; fold into ice cream mixture. Spoon into an angel food cake pan. Sprinkle surface lightly with almonds and powdered sugar. Cover with plastic wrap. Freeze until firm, about 4 to 5 hours or overnight. Unmold onto cold platter. Return to freezer until serving time.

HOT STRAWBERRY SAUCE:

1 quart fresh strawberries, cleaned and halved or 3 (10-ounce) packages frozen sliced strawberries

Sugar (about ½ cup for fresh berries, less for frozen)
5 tablespoons Grand Marnier

Just before serving, put berries in a saucepan with sugar; simmer until soft, but not mushy. Remove from heat; stir in Grand Marnier. Serve frozen soufflé topped with sauce. Yield: 12 servings.

Out of this World

Home-Made Ice Cream

6 eggs
1 cup sugar
4 tablespoons white corn syrup
1 (14-ounce) can sweetened
 condensed milk

1 teaspoon vanilla
Milk to fill a gallon freezer
 container to within 4 inches of
 top

Beat eggs and sugar into an electric mixer, then add other ingredients. Pour into container and freeze (by hand or electric) immediately according to freezer directions. After freezing, let set packed in ice for 30 minutes to 1 hour before serving. Makes 1 gallon.

VARIATIONS:

Pink Peppermint: Use basic recipe above omitting vanilla and adding: ½ teaspoon peppermint flavoring, 1 large stick (6-ounces) peppermint candy crushed, and red food coloring.

Chocolate Chip: Use basic recipe above and add: 1 large bar (8-ounces) of slivered chocolate candy.

Maple Nut: Use basic recipe omitting vanilla and adding: 2 teaspoons maple flavoring and 1½ cups toasted chopped pecans.

Fruit: Add about 1 quart of any sweetened fruit to the basic recipe

Daddy Special: Use basic recipe omitting vanilla and adding: 1 large slivered chocolate candy bar, 1 stick crushed peppermint candy, ½ teaspoon peppermint flavoring, 1 cup coconut, 1 cup miniature marshmallows and red food coloring.

The Nashville Cookbook

Aunt Clara's Peach Ice Cream

2 cups fresh peaches
1½–3 cups sugar to taste
3 whole eggs
2 teaspoons vanilla

1 quart milk (including 1 large
can evaporated milk)
2 cups whipping cream, whipped

Purée the peaches or mash well with a fork. Let stand an hour or two with sugar to sweeten. Mix eggs, some sugar, vanilla, and milk. Fold in whipped cream and peaches and freeze in freezer.

When freezing, remember to fill the barrel about ⅓ full of ice, and then pour in a layer of ice cream salt. Pour more ice, then more salt. Keep the freezer full of ice, but be careful that no salty water gets into the freezing container. When you have turned until hard, remove dasher, and pack tightly with ice and salt to ripen and harden. Or you can remove container to your own freezer. Serve when hard.

Chattanooga Cook Book

Pistachio Ice Cream

1 tablespoon flour
⅛ teaspoon salt
1 cup sugar
2 cups milk
1 egg

1 quart cream
1 teaspoon almond flavoring
½ teaspoon vanilla
¼ cup pistachio nuts
Green coloring

Mix flour, salt and sugar. Add scalded milk gradually and cook in a double boiler 20 minutes, stirring constantly until thickened. Add beaten egg and cook a few minutes longer. Cool; add cream, flavorings, nuts (which have been blanced and chopped) and coloring to make a delicate green. Pack in ice and salt; freeze. Serves 12.

Our Favorite Recipes

Ice Cream Hawaii

6 eggs
2 cups sugar
1 quart whipping cream or 1
  pint cream and 1 pint half-
  and-half
Juice of 2 lemons

Juice of 2 oranges
1 (8-ounce) can crushed
  pineapple, not drained
2 bananas, cubed
Dash of salt
1 teaspoon vanilla

Beat eggs and sugar until light. In separate bowl, whip cream. Mix both mixtures together in a very large bowl; add lemon and orange juices, pineapple, bananas, salt, and vanilla. Pour in electric or hand-operated freezer. Yields 1 gallon.

Gazebo Gala

Accompaniments

Antique memorabelia in one of the many century-old buildings in the quaint little town of Bell Buckle.

Sweet Crisp Green Tomato Pickles

8 pounds green tomatoes
2 cups lime (from builders
  supply)
2 gallons water
9 cups sugar

5–8 cups apple cider vinegar
1 tablespoon salt
10 drops green food color
  (optional)

Cut tomatoes into ½-inch slices. Mix lime and water; pour over tomatoes. Let stand for 24 hours. Rinse well and soak in cold water for 2 hours. Mix sugar, vinegar, salt and food coloring. Drain tomatoes and add to the sugar/vinegar mix. Soak tomatoes in mixture overnight. Bring to boil and boil for 40 minutes. Pack in clean hot jar and seal. Yield: 8 pints.

The Original Tennessee Homecoming Cookbook

Kosher Dill Pickles

Small cucumbers
Dill
Crushed red pepper
Garlic

20 cups water
1 cup vinegar (cider)
1 cup Kosher non-iodized salt
Alum

Scrub small cucumbers (must be fresh) in cold water. In dish-washed or sterilized quart jars, put 1 clove of garlic, ½ teaspoon red pepper, a little dill. Pack cucumbers in jar as tightly as possible, putting pieces of dill intermittently. Add one more clove of garlic, ½ teaspoon red pepper, a little more dill, 1 teaspoon salt. Fill jars 1 inch from top. Make brine with 20 cups water, 1 cup cider vinegar, and 1 cup salt. When brine is boiling, pour over jars of cucumbers, one at a time, sealing each immediately with hot sterilized lids and rims. For winter pickles, add a piece of alum (the size of a pea) to each jar before adding boiling brine. Pickles take approximately 3 weeks to ferment.

NCJW Cookbook

Bread & Butter Pickles

1 gallon sliced cucumbers	4 cups sugar
12 small onions, sliced	1½ teaspoons tumeric
½ cup salt	½ teaspoon cloves
Cracked ice	1 teaspoon celery seed
4 cups vinegar	2 teaspoons mustard seed

Let cucumbers and onions stand for 3 hours in salted ice water. Bring to a boil vinegar, sugar, tumeric, cloves, celery seed and mustard seed. Add cucumbers and onions. Simmer until they lose their bright color. Seal in jars.

Cracker Barrel Old Country Stores:
Old Timey Recipes & Proverbs to Live By

Apple Relish
Excellent!

14 large apples (Winesaps are
  good not peeled)
1 large bunch celery
6 red bell peppers

6 green bell peppers
12 onions
1 quart vinegar
6 cups sugar

Put apples and vegetables through food chopper.
Combine with vinegar and sugar and cook (boil) 15 minutes.
Can and seal. Yield: 8 to 10 pints.

Sam Houston Schoolhouse Cookbook

Chow Chow

1 gallon chopped cabbage
12 onions
12 green peppers (sweet)
12 red peppers (sweet)
2 quarts chopped green
  tomatoes
4 tablespoons ground mustard
1 tablespoon tumeric

1 tablespoon ground ginger
4 tablespoons mustard seed
3 tablespoons celery seed
2 tablespoons mixed whole
  spices
5 cups sugar
2 to 3 quarts vinegar

Chop onion and peppers. Mix all vegetables with ½ cup salt. Let
stand overnight. Drain. Tie the mixed spices in a bag. Add sugar
and spices to the vinegar. Simmer for 20 minutes. Add all the other
ingredients and simmer until hot and well seasoned. (10 minutes).
Remove the spice bag. Pack chow chow into hot sterilized jars and
seal at once. Makes 14 pints.

Cracker Barrel Old Country Stores:
Old Timey Recipes & Proverbs to Live By

Hot Pepper Jelly

4 large bell peppers (1⅓ pounds)	1½ cups white vinegar
½ cup fresh hot red peppers (12)	Green food coloring (6–8 drops)
or 4 tablespoons crushed dried	2 (6-ounce) bottles liquid pectin
red peppers	
7 cups sugar	

In large pot, place peppers that have been ground fine, (use juice and pulp), sugar and vinegar. Bring to full boil; reduce heat to low and simmer 10 minutes. Add green food coloring and pectin. Stir well. Bring mixutre to a boil over high heat; reduce heat and boil 1 minute. Remove from heat and pour mixture into hot dry, sterilized half-pint jars. Seal while hot. Makes 8 pints. To use as hor d'oeuvre, spread crackers with cream cheese and top with dab of pepper jelly. This is great!

Rivertown Recipes

Apricot Mustard

Soak 1 box medium size apricots in cold water to cover for 1 hour. Cover saucepan, cook apricots for 10 minutes, or until soft. Mash them and juice through a fine sieve, or purée in blender. To each 1½ cups purée add:

1½ teaspoons curry powder	2 tablespoons dry mustard
3 tablespoons honey	1 teaspoon powdered ginger
1 teaspoon almond extract	2–3 tablespoons sweet sherry

Blend well. Yield: 1 pint.
   Excellent with cold meats or poultry.

Woman's Exchange Cookbook I

Dillondown Bar-B-Q Sauce
for Pork Chops or Pork Ribs

½ cup apricot preserves
1 cup catsup
2 tablespoons prepared mustard
1 tablespoon A-1 sauce
1 tablespoon Worcestershire
  sauce

1 teaspoon garlic powder
1 teaspoon black pepper
½ cup brown sugar or molasses
½ cup cider vinegar
1 onion
Tops of 4 celery stalks

Put all ingredients in blender and blend well. Brown meat on grill, then baste frequently with sauce. Cook slowly until tender.

For variation, substitute pineapple preserves for apricot; and add 1 teaspoon ginger.

Gazebo Gala

Butternut Sauce

½ cup chocolate sauce   ¼ cup crunchy peanut butter

Combine sauce and peanut butter. Heat to melt peanut butter. (A microwave oven is great for this.) Pour over pound cake while sauce is warm.

Hint: This sauce is also good over ice cream, angel food cake, and fruit (try it with baked pears).

More Home Cooking in a Hurry

Chocolate Gravy

3 tablespoons cocoa
¾ cup sugar

1 tablespoon flour
2 cups milk (or water)

Mix cocoa, sugar and flour in a skillet; stir in milk or water. Cook on medium heat until mixture thickens, stirring continuously. Serve with hot biscuits and butter. Also great on pancakes.

Cookin' & Quiltin'

Index

Elvis Presley's statue looks out over Beale Street in downtown Memphis, where he maintained his home throughout his career.

INDEX

INDEX

INDEX

INDEX

INDEX

INDEX

Catalog of
Contributing
Cookbooks

Picturesque Big South Fork River in Pickett State Park, one of over 50 state parks in Tennessee.

All recipes in this book have been submitted from the Tennessee cookbooks shown on the following pages. Individuals who wish to obtain a copy of any particular book can do so by sending a check or money order to the addresses listed. Prices are subject to change. Please note the postage and handling charges that are required. Tennessee residents add tax only when requested. Retailers are invited to call or write to same address for wholesale information.

...AND GARNISH WITH MEMORIES
by Patty Smithdeal Fulton
P. O. Box 1261
Johnson City, TN 37605   615/926-2691

Author Patty Fulton reveals a warm, outgoing personality in her homey discussion throughout the volume, with nearly 600 recipes included as a part of the conversation. Here is a volume to be treasured. 290 pages. Spiral bound.

$14.95 Retail price
$ 1.16 Tax for Tennessee residents
$ 1.00 Postage and handling
Make check payable to The Overmountain Press
ISBN 0-932807-13-5

THE APPLE BARN COOKBOOK
Riverbend Farm
230 Lonesome Valley Road
Sevierville, TN 37862   615/453-9319

An apple a day, cooked our way! Find out all about the versatility of the apple as we share with you family recipes for apple pies, desserts, main dishes, salads, apple butter, jellies, and other apple treats. Also tips on how to treat apples. A must for your cookbook collection. 94 pages.

$5.95 Retail price
$1.25 Postage and handling
Make check payable to The Apple Barn
ISBN 0-9611508

CHANGE OF SEASONS

Department of Nutrition Services
Vanderbilt University Medical Center
Nashville, TN 37232   615/322-2321

Much more than a cookbook, *Change of Seasons* contains recipes, healthy eating guidelines, and weight loss hints. Persons following low salt/sodium diets or health professionals teaching low sodium/salt regimens will find this an excellent reference.

$10.00 Retail price
Make check payable to VUMC Dept. of Nutrition Services

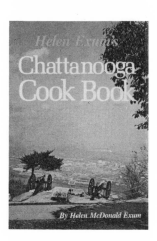

CHATTANOOGA COOK BOOK

by Helen McDonald Exum
400 East 11th Street
Chattanooga, TN 37401-1447   615/756-6900

This book reads like a historical novel set in Chattanooga, Tennessee. Chattanooga cooks, bits of history, chatty stories about the southern dishes popular in this region. Amply illustrated with pictures of Chattanooga people and places, this is Chattanooga's best selling book.

$12.95 Retail price
$ .94 Tax for Tennessee residents
$ 2.00 Postage and handling
Make check payable to *Chattanooga Cook Book*

COOKIN' & QUILTIN' WITH THE JOLLY DOZEN

by The Jolly Dozen Quilters
Route 1, Box 262
Linden, TN 37096   615/589-5278

Cookin' & Quiltin' with the Jolly Dozen contains over 200 favorite recipes and quilt patterns in 137 pages. This group of ladies in Middle Tennessee has been *Cookin' & Quiltin'* for 35 years. They would like to share with you, "good eatin' and good quiltin'." They hope you enjoy it.

$9.95 Retail price
$2.00 Postage and handling
Make check payable to The Jolly Dozen

CRACKER BARREL OLD COUNTRY STORES: OLD TIMEY RECIPES & PROVERBS TO LIVE BY
by Phila Hach
P. O. Box 787 Hartmann Dr.
Lebanon, TN 37088   615/444-0040

Here's a book that's any Southerner's choice. It is full of good southern country recipes and proverbs which will help make any day special. You can enjoy those memories of old fashioned goodness when you read and use this book. We at the Cracker Barrel Old Country Store do what we can to preserve those memories. 144 pages.

$6.99 Retail price
$ .49 Tax for Tennessee residents
$2.00 Postage and handling
Make check payable to Cracker Barrel Old Country Store
ISBN 09606192-1-6

DAS GERMANTOWN KOCHBUCH
by Evelyn Kempson and Edythe Connelly
1227-7th Avenue, North
Nashville, TN 37208   615/256-2729

Published in 1980 by two historic churches of Nashville, a Catholic and Methodist church in the old Germantown community, this best seller is in its second edition. 335 recipes. 273 pages. It has more than local appeal—into it have gone the wisdom and skill of European ancestors who knew German food at its best.

$10.00 Retail price
$ 1.50 Postage and handling
Make check payable to Church of the Assumption

DINNER ON THE DINER
Junior League of Chattanooga, Publications
100 Stivers Street
Chattanooga, TN 37405   615/267-5053

Sporting a shiny red vinyl-coated 3-D ring binder, *Dinner on the Diner* is easy to read and lies flat. Thirteen local artists portray Chattanooga's beautiful mountain tops and valleys with lovely illustrations. There are 650 thoroughly edited and triple tested recipes in this 414-page book with a comprehensive cross index.

$15.95 Retail price
$ 1.15 Tax for Tennessee residents
$ 1.75 Postage and handling
Make check payable to JLC Publications
ISBN 0-9611806-0-9

DIXIE DELIGHTS

St. Francis Hospital Auxiliary
P. O. Box 171808
Memphis, TN 38119   901/765-1831

A distinctive cookbook characteristic of Memphis and the Mid-South with 500 personally tested recipes. There are 27 black and white photographs showing Memphis landmarks and points of interest. Full color, durable hard cover; helpful hints marked with cotton balls throughout the book.

$9.95 Retail price
$ .77 Tax for Tennessee residents
$1.50 Postage and handling
Make check payable to St. Francis Hospital Auxiliary
ISBN 0-939114-79-8

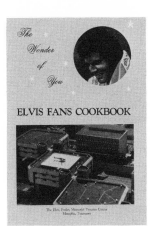

ELVIS FANS COOKBOOK

Edited by Wilma K. Wooten
P. O. Box 238
Welcome, NC 27374   919/764-3131 or 764-2472

In 236 pages, these 670 recipes are from Elvis' fans all over the United States and seven foreign countries. The 10 indexed categories feature illustrations and photographs depicting various stages of Elvis' life. All profits are used for life-saving equipment purchases for the Elvis Presley Memorial Trauma Center in Memphis.

$5.00 Retail price
$1.25 Postage and handling
Make check payable to Elvis Fans Cookbook

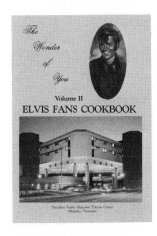

ELVIS FANS COOKBOOK— VOLUME II

Edited by Wilma K. Wooten
P. O. Box 238
Welcome, NC 27374   919/764-3131 or 764-2472

Here are 548 favorite recipes from Elvis' fans, including special celebrity section. Elvis' "Fried Peanut Butter Sandwich" is included as well as favorites from well-known entertainers, songwriters, individuals associated with Elvis and many others. A fund-raising project to benefit the Elvis Presley Memorial Trauma Center in Memphis. 224 pages.

$6.50 Retail price
$1.50 Postage and handling
Make check payable to Elvis Fans Cookbook

ENCORE! NASHVILLE

Nashville Junior League Publications
2202 Crestmoor Road
Nashville, TN 37215   615/269-4128

This book is perfect for the gift-giver and cookbook collector, and it is IRRESISTIBLE to the country music fan! Featured are autographs and recipes of 28 of Nashville's most popular country music stars, from Dolly Parton to Alabama. Each recipe is rated for ease of preparation and preparation time.

$12.50 Retail price
$ .97 Tax for Tennessee residents
$ 1.50 Postage and handling
Make check payable to Nashville Junior League Publications
ISBN 0-939114-68-2

FAMILY FAVORITES BY THE MILLER'S DAUGHTERS

by Harva U. Thomas & Christine U. Kyte
Rt. 1, Box 289
Kodak, TN 37764   615/933-2202

This cookbook contains our favorite kitchen-tested, family and friend-approved recipes. Some have been handed down through several generations. This collection of 300 recipes, by two sisters, has 112 pages plus 50 pages of helpful hints. Recipes that are easy to prepare, and the taste is good old country cooking.

$6.95 Retail price
$1.00 Postage and handling
Make check payable to Harva U. Thomas

FLAUNTING OUR FINEST

Franklin Junior Auxiliary
P. O. Box 541
Franklin, TN 37065   615/794-0665

Finally, a successful blend of past and present, uniquely presented in a cookbook for all ages. Beautifully illustrated with pencil drawings of many of the restored homes in this picturesque Tennessee town, the book contains over 600 recipes for all occasions. A cookbook that will grace any kitchen, *Flaunting Our Finest* is the perfect gift.

$9.95 Retail price
$1.55 Postage and handling
Make check payable to Franklin Junior Auxiliary
ISBN 0-939-114-76-3

GATLINBURG RECIPE COLLECTION
by Nancy Blanche Cooper
Rt. 3 The Woodlands—106
Gatlinburg, TN 37738   615/436-4639

Gatlinburg Recipe Collection came out April 1986, and features 125 pages of recipes from cooks in Gatlinburg and the Smoky Mountain area. This is the first printing and my first book, and with the success of this first year, I hope to do a number 2 book sometime soon.

$6.95 Retail price
$2.00 Postage and handling
Make check payable to Nancy B. Cooper

GAZEBO GALA
McMinnville Junior Auxiliary
P. O. Box 791
McMinnville, TN 37110

ATTENTION ALL COOKS AND COLLECTORS: *Gazebo Gala* is so eye-appealing and contains 640 excellent recipes and menus from McMinnville's best cooks and their friends. There is a front directory for each section, easy-to-read directions, plastic binding so that it falls open easily and a detailed index. 255 pages.

$9.95 Retail price
$2.00 All related costs
Make check payable to McMinnville Junior Auxiliary

GRAND TOUR COLLECTION
The Tennessee Chapter of
The American Society of Interior Designers
160 South McLean at Union
Memphis, TN 38104   901/274-9263

This lovely book reflects the "good taste" of interior designers, not only in its wonderful recipes but in the beautiful artwork and renderings depicting international dining scenes. Also features Artistry with Napkins with 12 illustrated pages of folding techniques, plus household hints. Indexed. 400 pages.

$11.95 Retail price
$ .80 Tax for Tennessee residents
$ 1.50 Postage and handling
Make checks payable to The Tennessee A.S.I.D., Cookbook
ISBN 0-939114-21-6

HOME COOKING IN A HURRY

by Sarah Howell
Baptist Book Center—Mail Order Center
P. O. Box 24420
Nashville, TN 37202   615/251-2094

This book is for those who want to make use of time spent in the kitchen, so they and their families will not miss the joys of home cooking and warm hospitality; people who want good, delicious food on the table with the least amount of time and effort. Indexed. Hard cover.

$7.95 Retail price
$ .56 Tax for Tennessee residents
$1.50 Postage and handling
Make check payable to Baptist Book Center
ISBN 0-8054-7002-6

IT'S GREEK TO ME!

Annunciation Greek Orthodox Church
P. O. Box 22764
Memphis, TN 38122   901/327-8177

Cover in full color, picture of a church in Greek Islands across both front & back covers; plastic combspine, 174 pages; divided into categories (appetizers, soups, salads, etc.). A section devoted to basic techniques—including sketches; wines and cheeses; index by category with ethnic title and English translation.

$7.95 Retail price
$ .61 Tax for Tennessee residents
$1.50 Postage and handling
Make check payable to Annunciation Greek Orthodox Church

THE JAMES K. POLK COOKBOOK

James K. Polk Memorial Association Auxiliary
301 West Seventh Street
Columbia, TN 38401   615/388-2354 or 388-9620

A mixture of recipes and history provides both interesting reading and cooking. 254 pages, 600 tested recipes, with durable Stacon covers and plastic comb binding. This book contains personal notes and recipes from recent First Ladies, Bess Truman through Nancy Reagan, and is a treasure of past and present Southern recipes.

$8.95 Retail price
$ .69 Tax for Tennessee residents
$1.25 Postage and handling
Make check payable to *James K. Polk Cookbook*
ISBN 9607668-04

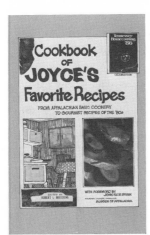

JOYCE'S FAVORITE RECIPES

Edited by Robert L. Breeding
3328 Cunningham Road
Knoxville, TN 37918

The first 30 pages of this cookbook describes basic Appalachian cookery of the 1930's and contains the ole-time recipes for such basics as cornbread, grits, biscuits, cracklin' bread, and chicken and dumplings. The remainder of the cookbook contains more than 500 gourmet recipes gathered from all over the world. Beautifully hardbound.

$10.00 Retail price
$ .70 Tax for Tennessee residents
$ 1.00 Postage and handling
Make check payable to Robert L. Breeding

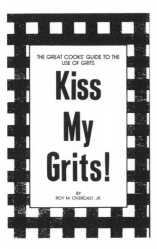

KISS MY GRITS

by Roy M. Overcast, Jr.
2301 12th Avenue South
Nashville, TN 37204   615/297-6770

Kiss My Grits, the great cooks' guide to the use of grits, is a composite of over 55 recipes Southerners share with you. Their home-tested recipes and expertise on the use of grits as a tasty and international food will expand your horizons and loosen your creativity on the use of grits as an exciting food.

$6.00 Retail price
$ .47 Tax for Tennessee residents
$1.00 Postage and handling
Make check payable to Roy Overcast
ISBN 84-90660

KOINONIA COOKING

by Elaine S. Mynatt
Elm Publications
P. O. Box 23192
Knoxville, TN 37933   615/966-5703

"An experience in fellowship . . . recipes collected from members and friends of Central Baptist Church of Bearden, Knoxville, Tennessee." As entertaining to read as it is delicious to cook from! Cartoon illustrations by artist Gale Lee. Over 300 recipes.

$6.00 Retail price
$ .49 Tax for Tennessee residents
$1.00 Postage and handling
Make check payable to Elm Publications
ISBN 0-911175-00-8

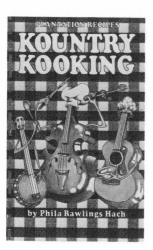

KOUNTRY KOOKING
by Phila R. Hach
1601 Madison Street
Clarksville, TN 37043   615/647-4084

An absolutely delightful book of great Southern country favorites. Red and white checked with unusual art drawings.

$9.95 Retail price
$ .77 Tax for Tennessee residents
$1.50 Postage and handling
Make check payable to Phila R. Hach
ISBN 0-9606192-2-4

A MAN'S TASTE
Junior League of Memphis
2711 Union Avenue Extended
Memphis, TN 38112   901/452-2151

A collection of tasty recipes written by men for the best of culinary tastes. Not only does this clever book contain recipes for barbecue sauces, wild game, grilled steaks, and hamburgers, but the haughtiest of haute cuisine— cold soups, salads, and light pastries.

$7.95 Retail price
$ .61 Tax for Tennessee residents
$1.50 Postage and handling
Make check payable to Memphis Junior League Publications
ISBN 0-960422-2-6

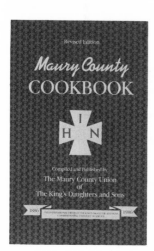

MAURY COUNTY COOKBOOK
The Maury County Union of
King's Daughters & Sons
412 West 9th Street
Columbia, TN 38401   615/388-3810

In this new cookbook there is a combining of the elegance of the Old South with the efficiency of the New. Some bits of history of The King's Daughters and Sons are included on divider pages. 276 pages and over 1000 recipes.

$12.95 Retail price
$ 3.00 Postage and handling
Make check payable to Maury County Cookbook Fund

THE MEMPHIS COOKBOOK

Junior League of Memphis
2711 Union Avenue Extended
Memphis, TN 38112   901/452-2151

The Memphis Cookbook, a bestseller since 1952, includes over 700 tasted and tested recipes. Great ideas for cooking have made this cookbook one of the top cookbook sellers. As Craig Claiborne, *New York Times* Food Editor says, it is "one of the best regional cookbooks in America."

$8.95 Retail price
$ .69 Tax for Tennessee residents
$1.50 Postage and handling
Make check payable to Memphis Junior League Publications
ISBN 0-960422-0-X

MINNIE PEARL COOKS

by Minnie Pearl
c/o Minnie Pearl's Museum
1500 Division Street
Nashville, TN 37203   615/256-4734

A delightful book with approximately 400 recipes from the famous Grand Ole Opry comedianne. Included with the delicious recipes from Minnie and her friends is autobiographical info, colorful pictures of Grand Ole Opry stars and cute anecdotes and stories. Good Tennessee cooking! Each book may be personally autographed by Minnie.

$8.95 Retail price
$ .69 Tax for Tennessee residents
$2.00 Postage and handling
Make check payable to Minnie Pearl's Museum

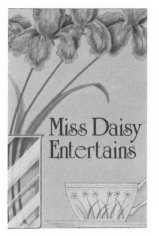

MISS DAISY ENTERTAINS

Miss Daisy's Restaurant
4029 Hillsboro Road
Nashville, TN 37215

"Lunch at Miss Daisy's" has become something of a tradition in middle Tennessee. Located in a large townhouse built in 1910, it has been the scene of many festive luncheons. Compiled by Marilyn Lehew and Daisy King, this companion to their first cookbook, *Recipes from Miss Daisy's,* contains delightful recipes served at the tearoom.

$6.95 Retail price
$ .54 Tax for Tennessee residents
$1.50 Postage and handling
Make check payable to Miss Daisy's Restaurant
ISBN 0-934395-16-0

MORE HOME COOKING IN A HURRY

by Sarah Howell
Baptist Book Center—Mail Order Center
P. O. Box 24420
Nashville, TN 37202   615/251-2094

Written with singles, couples, and small families in mind, the book features breakfast ideas for people on the go, sack lunch menus and recipes, and how to use time-saving appliances to simplify meals (including freezer, food processor, and microwave oven.) Cheese chart. Indexed. Hard cover.

$7.95 Retail price
$ .56 Tax for Tennessee residents
$1.50 Postage and handling
Make check payable to Baptist Book Center
ISBN 0-8054-7003-4

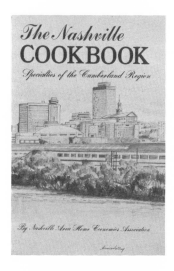

THE NASHVILLE COOKBOOK

Nashville Area Home Economics Association
Box 120324 Acklen Station
Nashville, TN 37212   615/889-2482

The Nashville Cookbook is a sampler of the best of Nashville, from the pioneer period to the present, on 331 plus pages. It is a collection of 676 traditional and currently favored recipes; a showcase of collectors' prints with brief history of historical Nashville; and, contains a special dietary section by nutritionist-dietitians.

$10.00 Retail price
$ .50 Tax for Tennessee residents
$ 1.50 Postage and handling
Make check payable to *The Nashville Cookbook*

NASHVILLE SEASONS

Nashville Junior League Publications
2202 Crestmoor Road
Nashville, TN 37215   615/269-4128

Authentic menus at the beginning set the stage for the Southern elegance throughout this book. Over 900 delectable Tennessee recipes. Originally published over 20 years ago, *Nashville Seasons* is now in its 11th printing. Revised in 1984, this updated classic comes with washable cover and spiral lay-flat binding. Gift wrapping available free of charge.

$12.50 Retail price
$ .97 Tax for Tennessee residents
$ 1.50 Postage and handling
Make check payable to Nashville Junior League Publications
ISBN 0-9611076-0-X

NCJW COOKBOOK

Members of Nashville Section
National Council of Jewish Women
c/o J.C.C. 801 Percy Warner Blvd.
Nashville, TN 37205   615/352-0864

This is the second edition of selected recipes of local members of the Nashville Section of the National Council of Jewish Women and the best of the original *NCJW Nashville Section Cookbook.* Included are traditional Jewish recipes and everything from hors d' oeuvres to pickles, preserves and desserts. Over 600 recipes. 314 pages.

$10.00 Retail price
$ .78 Tax for Tennessee residents
$ 1.25 Postage and handling
Make check payable to NCJW

THE ORIGINAL TENNESSEE HOMECOMING COOKBOOK

Edited by Daisy King
Rutledge Hill Press
513 Third Avenue South
Nashville, TN 37210   615/244-2700

A collection of favorite recipes from Tennessee kitchens, from traditional southern cooking of the foods "everybody grew up eating" to New South sophisticated cuisine. Has become a bestseller from coast to coast and border to border. 240 pages; 518 recipes; 39 full-color photographs. Introduction on Tennesseans and food by Helen McDonald Exum.

$14.95 Retail price
$ 1.16 Tax for Tennessee residents
$ 1.75 Postage and handling
Make check payable to Rutledge Hill Press
ISBN 0-934395-05-5

OUR FAVORITE RECIPES

The South Carolina Club of Bethel AME Church
2460 Parkview Avenue
Knoxville, TN 37917   615/522-6396

This 254-page spiral-bound, easy-to-read recipe book contains over 600 recipes and pages of household hints, with a combination of the practical and unusual recipes collected from friends and relatives from several different states.

$10.00 Retail price
$ 1.00 Postage and handling
Make check payable to The South Carolina Club of Bethel AME Church

OUT OF THIS WORLD
The Oak Hill School Parents' Association
4815 Franklin Road
Nashville, TN 37220   615/297-6544

"Oak Hill Parents' recipe collection is just 'Heavenly'"
and "there's an especially good chapter on hors
d'oeuvres," says Beverly Garrison, *Tennessean* Food Editor. The spiral-bound, Mylar-covered book contains
nearly 800 recipes in 366 pages with adorable and amus-
ing illustrations throughout. Easy-to-read format with
valuable culinary hints.

$10.00 Retail price
$ .78 Tax for Tennessee residents
$ 2.00 Postage and handling
Make check payable to Oak Hill Cook Book

PALATE PLEASERS
Forest Hills United Methodist Church
Old Hickory Boulevard
Brentwood, TN 37027   615/373-3131

Palate Pleasers is a collection of favorite recipes from
friends and relatives of the people of Forest Hills United
Methodist Church. In more than 300 pages, the recipes
are guaranteed to "please the palate."

$10.00 Retail price
$ 1.50 Postage and handling
Make check payable to Forest Hills United Methodist
Church

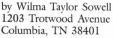

PARTIES & PLEASURES
by Wilma Taylor Sowell
1203 Trotwood Avenue
Columbia, TN 38401   615/388-9291

From her 20 years as a caterer, Wilma Sowell shares her
personal collection of over 450 recipes along with menus
and practical tips for party-planning. Includes food defi-
nitions, measurements, amounts needed to serve 100,
and party-giver's checklist. 173 pages, cross-referenced
index, 10 full-color photos, spiral-bound, softcover.

$10.95 Retail price
$ .85 Tax for Tennessee residents
$ 2.00 Postage and handling
Make check payable to Wilma Sowell Cookbook

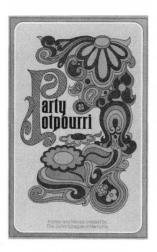

PARTY POTPOURRI

Junior League of Memphis
2711 Union Avenue Extended
Memphis, TN 38112   901/452-2151

Party Potpourri is a classic that can not only guide you to create that perfect dish, but can help you with food decorations and garnishes, preserving cut flowers and foliage for a centerpiece, and setting your table. A must for anyone who enjoys entertaining.

$8.95 Retail price
$ .69 Tax for Tennessee residents
$1.50 Postage and handling
Make check payable to Memphis Junior League Publications

RECIPES *from* MISS DAISY'S

Carter's Court, Franklin, Tennessee
H.G. Hill Center, Nashville, Tennessee

RECIPES FROM MISS DAISY'S

Miss Daisy's Tearoom Restaurant
4029 Hillsboro Road
Nashville, TN 37215   615/269-5354

These "tried and true" recipes have been bidding customers back to Miss Daisy's Tearoom time and again to enjoy the wonderful lunches, pleasant atmosphere, and personal service. Miss Daisy herself greets each customer, giving them a feeling of not only being welcomed, but honored. A delightful cookbook!

$4.95 Retail price
$ .38 Tax for Tennessee residents
$1.50 Postage and handling
Make check payable to Miss Daisy's Restaurant
ISBN 0-934395-15-2

Rivertown Recipes

RIVERTOWN RECIPES

Kennedy Book Club
5038 Millbranch—P. O. Box 16084
Memphis, TN 38116   901/346-8213

Our best collection of 800 favored recipes on 242 pages. *Rivertown Recipes* is for those who love to cook and to share their culinary delights with family, friends and those passing through.

$6.00 Retail price
$ .47 Tax for Tennessee residents
$2.00 Postage and handling
Make check payable to Kennedy Book Club

ST. PAUL COOKS

St. Paul Christian Academy
5035 Hillsboro Road
Nashville, TN 37215   615/269-4751

279 pages of 900 mouth-watering recipes with the following categories: appetizers, soups, salads, vegetables, main dishes, breads, rolls, pastries, pies, cookies, cakes, desserts, candies, jellies, beverages, microwave, and miscellaneous. A great all-purpose cookbook, graced with delightful artwork of St. Paul students.

$9.95 Retail price
$ .79 Tax for Tennessee residents
$1.00 Postage and handling
Make check payable to St. Paul Christian Academy

SAM HOUSTON SCHOOLHOUSE COOKBOOK

Sam Houston Schoolhouse Association
P. O. Box 281
Maryville, TN 37803-0281   615/983-1550

Sam Houston Schoolhouse Cookbook skillfully combines cooking and history in 301 pages with 500 plus recipes of today and yesteryear. Drawings and information on sites on National Historic Registry add interest. Fifteen printings since 1980 prove it is an excellent cookbook.

$8.00 Retail price
$1.25 Postage and handling
Make check payable to Sam Houston Schoolhouse Assn.

THE SEVIER COUNTY COOKBOOK

Compiled by Patsy Bradford
2436 Long Branch Road
Seymour, TN 37865   615/453-5669

The Sevier County Cookbook is a 236-page sampler of 425 recipes for home-cooked meals from simple foods. Composed of recipes from Sevier County women, interlaced with historical facts about the county, it also contains artwork by David Peek and special sections on Holiday Favorites and "old timey" country fixin's.

$7.00 Retail price
$1.25 Postage and handling
Make check payable to Patsy Bradford

SMOKY MOUNTAIN MAGIC

Junior League of Johnson City, Inc.
High South Publications
P. O. Box 1082
Johnson City, TN 37605   615/928-4071

Now in its eighth printing, *Smoky Mountain Magic* has sold over 51,000 copies in 36 years. Includes sections of men's favorites (submitted by the men!) and East Tennessee favorites—the way Grandma used to cook! We trust you will relish the varied time-tested recipes and find some of our "Smoky Mountain Magic." 360 pages.

$8.50 Retail price
$ .64 Tax for Tennessee residents
$2.00 Postage and handling
Make check payable to High South Publications
ISBN 0-9616492-0-8

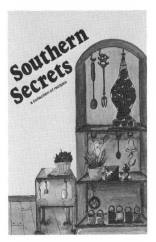

SOUTHERN SECRETS

The Episcopal Day School Mother's Club
Rt. #1 Old Humbolt Road
Jackson, TN 38305   901/668-8400

Over 400 recipes in 252 pages, contains party menus and recipes with plans, quick and easy section, terrific low-calorie menus and recipes with calorie count, hints helpful to cooks from novice to gourmet. Cross indexed; contains favorite and special family recipes with simple ingredients and easy-to-follow instructions.

$8.95 Retail price
$ .63 Tax for Tennessee residents
$1.55 Postage and handling
Make check payable to *Southern Secrets*
ISBN 0-918544-30-0

TENNESSEE HOMECOMING: FAMOUS PARTIES, PEOPLE & PLACES

by Phila R. Hach
1601 Madison Street
Clarksville, TN 37043   615/647-4084

A great cookbook filled with Tennessee's famous people, history, places & parties. Recipes by former American Airline stewardess, T.V. personality and caterer, Phila Hach.

$9.95 Retail price
$ .77 Tax for Tennessee residents
$1.50 Postage and handling
Make check payable to Phila Hach
ISBN 0-9606192-6-7

TENNESSEE'S 95 MAGIC MIXES: SECOND HELPING

American Cancer Society, Tennessee Division, Inc.
1315 8th Ave. S.
Nashville, TN 37203   615/255-1227

This book is chock-full of over 300 delicious "down home" recipes from all parts of the Volunteer State! There's even a Celebrity Chapter with recipes from such notables as Minnie Pearl, Ronnie Milsap, and Larry Gatlin. Full-color cover, indexed, and spiral bound. Use it for yourself or give it as a gift!

$10.00 Contribution
Make check payable to American Cancer Society

TENNESSEE TREASURE

by Pearlie B. Scott, MC Art Co.
P. O. Box 100905
Nashville, TN 37210

Over 650 prized recipes that were handed down by Tennessee families for over 100 years. Many recipes were donated in their original, handwritten form on yellowed paper with faded words that could hardly be read. Bound in heavy, bendable vinyl and decorated in the soft dove grey and violets of yesteryear, it is truly an heirloom.

$10.95 Retail price
$ .85 Tax for Tennessee residents
$ 1.50 Postage and handling
Make check payable to *Tennessee Treasure*

UPPER CRUST: A SLICE OF THE SOUTH

Junior League of Johnson City, Inc.
High School Publications
P. O. Box 1082
Johnson City, TN 37605   615-928-4071

Upper Crust provides a view of how we eat today, including a section of favorite recipes from local restaurants. There are 309 pages of recipes selected from over 1200 submissions. Many recipes (denoted by our symbol—a slice of blackberry pie) take less than 15 minutes preparation time.

$13.95 Retail price
$ 1.00 Tax for Tennessee residents
$ 2.00 Postage and handling
Make check payable to High South Publications
ISBN 0-9616492-1-6

WELL SEASONED

Les Passees Publications
40 South Idlewild
Memphis, TN 38104 901/272-1268

Well Seasoned, a 448-page cookbook, represents eight years of collecting and five years of taste testing. Over 2000 triple-tested recipes were finally narrowed to 800, yielding one of the most professionally produced collections of practical recipes available on the market today. Over 30,000 sold since June '82. Proceeds go to Les Passees Children's Rehabilitation Center.

$14.95 Retail Price
$ 1.16 Tax for Tennessee residents
$ 2.00 Postage and handling
Make check payable to Les Passees Publications
ISBN 0-939114-42-9

WOMAN'S EXCHANGE COOKBOOK—VOLUME I

Woman's Exchange
88 Racine Street
Memphis, TN 38111 901/327-5681

Woman's Exchange Cookbook—Volume I (red cover with print of Woman's Exchange building) has been popular all over the U.S. for many years, and is now in its sixth printing. A proven favorite. 272 pages. Approximately 1600 recipes.

$5.95 Retail price
$ .46 Tax for Tennessee residents
$1.00 Postage and handling
Make check payable to The Woman's Exchange, Inc.

WOMAN'S EXCHANGE COOKBOOK—VOLUME II

Woman's Exchange
88 Racine Street
Memphis, TN 38111 901/327-5681

Woman's Exchange Cookbook—Volume II (blue cover with white outlined print of the Woman's Exchange building) contains more outstanding proven favorite recipes. This book includes some "quickie" recipes for the busy homemaker and also a low calorie chapter. 272 pages. Approximately 1600 recipes.

$5.95 Retail price
$ .46 Tax for Tennessee residents
$1.00 Postage and handling
Make check payable to The Woman's Exchange, Inc.

600 International & Appalachian · Southern Recipes

OFFICIAL COOKBOOK
THE 1982 WORLD'S FAIR.
MAY · OCTOBER, 1982 KNOXVILLE, TENNESSEE

WORLD'S FAIR COOKBOOK
by Phila R. Hach
1601 Madison Street
Clarksville, TN 37043   615/647-4084

Over 600 recipes collected from around the world including a special section on Appalachian folklore and food. Over 100,000 copies sold, this is the official cookbook of the 1982 World's Fair held in Knoxville.

$9.00 Retail price
$ .70 Tax for Tennessee residents
$1.50 Postage and handling
Make check payable to Phila Hach
ISBN 0-9606192-0-8

The Quail Ridge Press "Best of the Best" Series:

Best of the Best from Louisiana $12.95   0-937552-13-5
Best of the Best from Texas $14.95   0-937552-14-3
Best of the Best from Florida $12.95   0-937552-16-X
Best of the Best from Mississippi $12.95   0-937552-09-7
Best of the Best from Tennessee $12.95   0-937552-20-8

The Quail Ridge Press Cookbook Series:

The Little Gumbo Book $6.95   0-937552-17-8
Hors D'Oeuvres Everybody Loves $5.95   0-937552-11-9
The Seven Chocolate Sins $5.95   0-937552-01-1
A Salad A Day $5.95   0-937552-02-X
Quickies for Singles $5.95   0-937552-03-8
The Twelve Days of Christmas Cookbook $5.95   0-937552-00-3
The Country Mouse Cheese Cookbook $5.95   0-937552-10-0

Send check or money order or VISA/MasterCard number with expiration date to:

Quail Ridge Press
P. O. Box 123
Brandon, MS 39042

Please add $1.50 postage and handling for first book; $0.50 per additional book. Gift wrap with enclosed card add $1.00. Mississippi residents add 6% sales tax.